Collins

SNAP
REVISION

LOVE AND RELATIONSHIPS
POETRY ANTHOLOGY

AQA GCSE 9-1 English Literature

IAN KIRBY

REVISE TRICKY
TOPICS IN A SNAP

Published by Collins
An imprint of HarperCollinsPublishers
1 London Bridge Street,
London, SE1 9GF

© HarperCollinsPublishers Limited 2018

9780008320096

First published 2018

10 9 8 7 6 5 4 3 2

British Library Cataloguing in Publication Data.

A CIP record of this book is available from the British Library.

Printed in United Kingdom.

Commissioning Editor: Gillian Bowman
Managing Editor: Craig Balfour
Author: Steve Eddy
Proofreader: Jill Laidlaw
Typesetting: Jouve
Cover designers: Kneath Associates and Sarah Duxbury
Production: Katharine Willard

ACKNOWLEDGEMENTS
p.26, Maura Dooley 'Letters From Yorkshire', from Sound Barrier: Poems 1982-2002 reprinted with permission of Bloodaxe Books. www.bloodaxebooks.com.; p.35, 'Walking Away' from Selected Poems by Cecil day Lewis reprinted by permission of Peters Fraser & Dunlop (www.petersfraserdunlop. com) on behalf of the Estate of Cecil Day Lewis; p.39, Charles Causley 'Eden Rock' from Collected Poems, Macmillan; p.43, Seamus Heaney 'Follower' from Opened Ground by permission of Faber and Faber Ltd, p.47, Simon Armitage 'Mother, any distance' from A Book of Matches by permission of Faber and Faber Ltd. p.51, Carol Ann Duffy 'Before You Were Mine' Copyright © Carol Ann Duffy. Reproduced by permission of Carol Ann Duffy c/o Rogers, Coleridge & White Ltd., 20 Powis Mews, London W11 1JN; p.55, Owen Sheers 'Winter Swans' Copyright © Owen Sheers 2005. Reproduced by permission of the author c/o Rogers, Coleridge & White Ltd., 20 Powis Mews, London W11 1JN; p.59, Daljit Nagra 'Singh Song!' from Look We Have Coming to Dover! by permission of Faber and Faber Ltd; p.64, Andrew Waterhouse's 'Climbing My Grandfather' by permission of The Rialto.
The author and publisher are grateful to the copyright holders for permission to use quoted materials and images.

Every effort has been made to trace copyright holders and obtain their permission for the use of copyright material. The author and publisher will gladly receive information enabling them to rectify any error or omission in subsequent editions. All facts are correct at time of going to press.

Contents

Poems

'When We Two Parted' by
Lord Byron   4

'Love's Philosophy' by
Percy Bysshe Shelley   8

'Porphyria's Lover' by
Robert Browning   12

Sonnet 29 – 'I think of thee!' by
Elizabeth Barrett Browning   18

'Neutral Tones' by Thomas Hardy   22

'Letters from Yorkshire' by Maura
Dooley   26

'The Farmer's Bride' by
Charlotte Mew   30

'Walking Away' by Cecil
Day Lewis   35

'Eden Rock' by Charles Causley   39

'Follower' by Seamus Heaney   43

'Mother, any distance' by
Simon Armitage   47

'Before You Were Mine' by
Carol Ann Duffy   51

'Winter Swans' by Owen Sheers   55

'Singh Song!' by Daljit Nagra   59

'Climbing My Grandfather'
by Andrew Waterhouse   64

Comparison

Comparing Poetry   68

Practice Questions   72

The Exam

Tips and Assessment Objectives   77

Planning a Poetry Response   79

Grade 5 Annotated Response   81

Grade 7+ Annotated Response   83

Glossary   85

Answers   90

When we two parted
In silence and tears,
Half broken-hearted
To sever for years,
5 Pale grew thy cheek and cold,
Colder thy kiss;
Truly that hour foretold
Sorrow to this.

The dew of the morning
10 Sank chill on my brow –
It felt like the warning
Of what I feel now.
Thy vows are all broken,
And light is thy fame;
15 I hear thy name spoken,
And share in its shame.

They name thee before me,
A knell in mine ear;
A shudder comes o'er me –
20 Why wert thou so dear?
They know not I knew thee,
Who knew thee too well –
Long, long shall I rue thee,
Too deeply to tell.

25 In secret we met –
In silence I grieve,
That thy heart could forget,
Thy spirit deceive.
If I should meet thee
30 After long years,
How should I greet thee? –
With silence and tears.

This poem is about...

two secret lovers who had to part; years later, the speaker hears that his lover has been involved in some kind of romantic scandal.

How does the first stanza present the lovers' parting?

The nouns 'silence and tears' present the lovers as not wanting to part and not knowing what to say. The idea of a difficult parting is emphasised by the violence of the verb 'sever'. The metaphor 'half broken-hearted' shows how upset they were. However, 'half' allows the phrase to be interpreted in different ways: it could show they weren't fully broken-hearted, suggesting the **brevity** of their affair, or it could imply that only one of the two lovers (the speaker) was actually upset.

Byron foreshadows how the speaker is betrayed by the lover: 'Truly that hour foretold / Sorrow to this'. In the description 'Pale grew thy cheek and cold, / Colder thy kiss', the adjective cold is repeated but its impact increased by altering it to a comparative adjective. At the time, the speaker saw it as a sign of the lover's upset (linked to death, like 'broken-hearted') but now the speaker interprets it as a sign of a lack of love.

How does the second stanza show the lover's betrayal?

Byron writes in a manner that allows his lines to be interpreted in two different ways, conveying how the speaker felt at the time and what he now suspects upon reflection. The description 'The dew of the morning / Sank chill on my brow' could capture the speaker's grief, using 'dew' to symbolise tears and emphasising the depth of the speaker's feelings by linking them to death in the verb phrase 'sank chill'. However, this phrase could also show the speaker's suspicion that the lover's feelings weren't as strong. This is emphasised by the phrase 'It felt like the warning / Of what I feel now'.

The lover's betrayal is confirmed on line 13, 'Thy vows are all broken', suggesting they made promises the lover did not keep. The 'vows' also indicate that she is married and has had an affair; possibly her relationship with the speaker was also adulterous, explaining why they had to part. The following line, 'And light is thy fame', suggests the lover's affair is being gossiped about (the abstract noun 'fame' is being used in a negative way, as in notorious). This is emphasised by the verbs in 'I hear thy name spoken' and the abstract noun in 'And share in its shame'. The sibilance highlights the fact that the speaker also feels ashamed, suggesting their love was also potentially scandalous.

How do the last two stanzas show the speaker's feelings about the lover?

A metaphor compares the lover's name to 'A knell in mine ear', suggesting the pain and unhappiness it causes the speaker. This adds to the poem's references to death, suggesting the death of the speaker's former feelings. The rhetorical question 'Why wert thou so dear?' suggests the speaker regrets falling in love. This is emphasised by the repetition in 'Long, long shall I **rue** thee', and the admission 'Who knew thee too well', suggesting the speaker knew the lover couldn't be trusted.

The speaker refers to the secrecy of their affair, 'They know not I knew thee, / [...] In secret we met', reinforcing the idea that it would also have been scandalous. The opening of the fourth stanza uses parallelism to contrast the past and present, replacing the plural pronoun 'we' with the singular 'I' to emphasise separation. The speaker accuses the lover of betrayal, 'That thy heart could forget, / Thy spirit deceive', using parallelism and metaphor to emphasise the extremity of the lover's cruelty.

Wondering what would happen if they met again, the speaker ends 'How should I greet thee? – / With silence and tears'. The last line echoes the second line. Whereas the speaker's grief was about not wanting to part, now he feels betrayed; similarly, the silence was related to not knowing what to say and now represents not wanting to speak to the lover.

How does the poem's form contribute to the way meaning is conveyed?

This lyric poem is arranged into four octaves. The poem uses alternate rhyme (*abab*) rather than rhyming couplets (*aabb*), perhaps to represent the idea of parting or that there was an obstacle between the speaker and the lover (either the lover's marriage or lack of love).

The second and third stanzas have a uniform metre, alternating six- and five-syllable lines. The longer lines are formed by two amphibrachs (the DEW of the MORning), while the shorter lines contain an iamb followed by an anapaest (sank CHILL on my BROW). Having a greater proportion of unstressed beats mirrors the poem's mood of sadness and loss.

The first and last stanzas (particularly stanza 1) have a less consistent rhythm with the stressed beats placed in different positions:

WHEN we two PARted

in SIlence and TEARS [...]

PALE grew thy CHEEKS and COLD

COLder thy KISS

As these stanzas focus more on the speaker's memory of their love and parting, perhaps Byron is trying to convey how the speaker is feeling unsettled or struggling with the memory.

Additional context to consider

The poem doesn't mention names or gender, allowing it to relate to a variety of experiences. The first-person narration makes the poem more intimate and intensifies the emotions. However, this also means that our impression of the lover is biased as it's based only on the speaker's perspective. The actual relationship is described in hindsight.

Particularly when placed in its early 19th-century context, the poem shows attitudes to marital affairs and implies that women were judged more harshly than men.

Poetic links

- Lack of love in 'Love's Philosophy', 'Neutral Tones' or 'The Farmer's Bride'.
- The end of a relationship in 'Neutral Tones'.
- A separated relationship in 'Letters from Yorkshire', 'Walking Away' or 'Eden Rock'.

Sample analysis

'When We Too Parted' and 'Letters from Yorkshire' present separated relationships very differently. Byron focuses on his speaker's feelings of suspicion and betrayal, 'That thy heart could forget, / Thy spirit deceive', using metaphor to imply the depth of the lover's cruelty. The parallelism, and the way the second verb sounds more accusatory, builds up his feelings to emphasise the degree to which the lover hurt the speaker.

In comparison, 'Letters from Yorkshire' focuses on a relationship that is more **platonic** and based around sharing. The lines 'he saw the first lapwings return and came / indoors to write to me, his knuckles singing' also use metaphor but here it suggests the pleasure he takes in writing to her. The image also links to his pain from the cold, suggesting her consideration for him just as he shows a mutual consideration by wanting to share his news of the 'first' lapwings.

Questions

QUICK TEST
1. How are the 'silence and tears' presented differently at the start and end of the poem?
2. Where does the speaker foreshadow the lover's betrayal?
3. What words show the lover is being gossiped about?
4. Where does the speaker show he regrets the relationship?

EXAM PRACTICE
Using one or two of the highlighted quotations to learn, write a paragraph exploring how Byron presents the pain of feeling betrayed.

LOVE'S PHILOSOPHY
by Percy Bysshe Shelley

The fountains mingle with the river
And the rivers with the ocean,
The winds of Heaven mix for ever
With a sweet emotion;
5 Nothing in the world is single;
All things by a law divine
In one another's being mingle –
Why not I with thine?

See the mountains kiss high Heaven,
10 And the waves clasp one another;
No sister-flower would be forgiven
If it disdain'd its brother:
And the sunlight clasps the earth,
And the moonbeams kiss the sea –
15 What are all these kisses worth,
If thou kiss not me?

This poem is about...

a man trying to convince a woman to be with him; philosophy refers to asking questions about a subject and presenting a rational argument.

How do the first four lines present love?

The poem presents an image of two things combining, 'The fountains mingle with the river', symbolising two people making love. Nature imagery presents it as something normal and this is emphasised by the next line continuing to describe the water cycle, 'And the rivers with the ocean'. The two images show a weaker source of water merging with a stronger force. This could be seen as a traditional representation of the two sexes and perhaps suggests the woman should not fear the man. The water imagery could also be seen as an **erotic** representation of bodily fluids being exchanged.

The poet continues using nature imagery to symbolise two lovers, 'The winds of Heaven mix for ever / With a sweet emotion', adding a reference to Heaven to suggest love is holy as well as natural. The speaker's word choices try to convince the woman to be with him. The adverbial phrase 'for ever' links to faithfulness, the adjective 'sweet' suggests purity or harmony and the abstract noun 'emotion' implies a genuine romantic love rather than lust.

How do lines 5–8 establish the speaker's argument?

The poet uses hyperbole as a persuasive technique: 'Nothing in the world is single'. Up to this point, the poem has featured one clause for every two lines. The fifth line is a clause on its own and this sudden shortness makes the idea that it's bad to be single stand out; it also mirrors the speaker's message by having the clause unusually isolated on one line, rather than it being made up of a pair of lines.

The speaker returns to the idea that love is holy: 'All things by a law divine / In one another's being mingle –'. The noun phrase 'law divine' implies God wants people to be together. The verb 'mingle' is repeated from line 1 and the phrase 'in one another's being' is a euphemism for sexual intercourse.

The dash creates a dramatic pause to emphasise the subsequent rhetorical question, 'Why not I with thine?' The words 'thine' and 'divine' are rhymed to reinforce the idea that making love would not be an immoral or unholy act. This line is much simpler than the rest of stanza 1 as it contains no descriptive language, perhaps to portray him as honest and straightforward or to present love and sex as uncomplicated.

How does the second stanza develop the speaker's argument?

The second stanza opens with an imperative, imploring the woman to see love in the same way he does: 'See the mountains kiss high Heaven, / And the waves clasp one another'. Again, the use of nature imagery presents love and sex as natural while references to religion present it as holy. The personification and the choice of verbs, 'kiss [...] clasp' (compared to 'mingle' and 'mix' in stanza 1), add a more physical aspect. This could represent the speaker's desire or his growing sexual frustration. The tone of persuasion is built up by the anaphora of 'And'.

The lines 'No sister-flower would be forgiven / If it disdain'd its brother' continue the nature imagery but the tone is more accusatory due to the verb **'disdain'** and the suggestion that her behaviour is unforgiveable. However, the use of 'sister' and 'brother' presents his love as harmless and platonic rather than sexual.

The nature images on lines 13–14 reflect the speaker's obsession with the woman. While the verbs 'clasp' and 'kiss' continue to encourage her to be with him, she is also presented as 'sunlight' and 'moonbeams' to his 'earth' and 'sea'. As the Earth revolves around the Sun and the sea's tides are affected by the Moon's gravity, these images suggest he cannot resist her or avoid the effect she has on him. The poem ends, like stanza 1, with a rhetorical question, 'What are all these kisses worth, / If thou kiss not me?', suggesting the world he has been describing is nothing without her.

How does the poem's form contribute to the way meaning is conveyed?

This lyric poem is organised into two octaves with an *abab* rhyme scheme, perhaps using alternate rhyme instead of couplets to represent how the lovers aren't together. Despite this clear structure, the poem doesn't follow a set metre. This discrepancy could link to how the speaker is trying to persuade the woman to sleep with him while also trying to seem romantic, natural and unthreatening.

The poem's rhythm is usually trochaic (NOthing IN the WORLD is SINgle). By **foregrounding** the stressed beats, the poet emphasises the speaker's attempt at persuasion. The lines with uneven syllables are slightly different. Lines 1, 3, 7, 11 and 12 open with an amphibrach, while lines 6, 8 and 13–16 end with a cretic. The poet uses stronger images for men and weaker images for women in the first stanza so the stressed and unstressed beats could represent men and women: their lack of fluidity and uniformity could represent how the speaker and his lover aren't together and acting in union.

Additional context to consider

The poem appears to be about a man and woman but no names are used, allowing the poem to be more universal. The use of the first person adds intimacy and immediacy to the speaker's feelings.

It is unclear whether the woman will not take the next step in their relationship or if they are not yet even lovers. The poem is written as an argument, seeking to persuade the woman. It acknowledges, and plays with, traditional gender roles in which the man was seen as stronger than the woman. The need to prove that love and sex are both natural and holy (alongside the poem's implicit reference to sex outside marriage) is best understood in the context of the early 19th century, which was when the poem was written (1819).

Shelley was a Romantic poet and this literary movement's focus on nature imagery can be seen throughout the poem.

Poetic links

- Lack of love in 'When We Two Parted', 'Neutral Tones' or 'The Farmer's Bride'.
- A problem in a relationship in 'Neutral Tones', 'The Farmer's Bride' or 'Winter Swans'.
- Romantic love in 'I think of thee!', 'Winter Swans' or 'Singh Song!'.
- Nature imagery in 'I think of thee!', 'Neutral Tones', 'The Farmer's Bride', 'Winter Swans' or 'Climbing My Grandfather'.
- Desire in 'The Farmer's Bride' or 'Singh Song!'.
- The use of extended metaphor in 'I think of thee!', 'Mother, any distance' or 'Climbing My Grandfather'.

Sample analysis

'Love's Philosophy' and 'When We Two Parted' present speakers who are without love. Shelley's speaker tries to convince a woman to be with him, 'See the mountains kiss high Heaven', using images of nature and references to religion to suggest that love and sex are normal and holy. The personification and the verb 'kiss' highlight the physical aspect of the relationship while the trochaic tetrameter emphasises the persistently persuasive tone.

In comparison, Byron's speaker reflects on a separation. The metaphor 'half broken-hearted' suggests the depth of his unhappiness. Because the relationship is described in hindsight after he has been betrayed by the woman, the additional adjective 'half' could suggest his suspicion that – of the two of them – only he felt heart-broken. Like Shelley, Byron's use of rhythm is important, with the larger proportion of unstressed beats reflecting the speaker's weakness and upset.

Questions

QUICK TEST
1. What does the nature imagery used suggest about love?
2. What do the references to religion suggest about love?
3. What technique is used at the end of both stanzas?
4. Which verbs link to joining or coupling?

EXAM PRACTICE
Using one or two of the highlighted quotations to learn, write a paragraph exploring how Shelley presents the speaker's love.

PORPHYRIA'S LOVER
by Robert Browning

The rain set early in to-night,
    The sullen wind was soon awake,
It tore the elm-tops down for spite,
    and did its worst to vex the lake:
5   I listened with heart fit to break.
When glided in Porphyria; straight
    She shut the cold out and the storm,
And kneeled and made the cheerless grate
    Blaze up, and all the cottage warm;
10   Which done, she rose, and from her form
Withdrew the dripping cloak and shawl,
    And laid her soiled gloves by, untied
Her hat and let the damp hair fall,
    And, last, she sat down by my side
15   And called me. When no voice replied,
She put my arm about her waist,
    And made her smooth white shoulder bare,
And all her yellow hair displaced,
    And, stooping, made my cheek lie there,
20   And spread o'er all her yellow hair,
Murmuring how she loved me – she
    Too weak, for all her heart's endeavour,
To set its struggling passion free
    From pride, and vainer ties dissever,
25   And give herself to me for ever.
But passion sometimes would prevail,
    Nor could tonight's gay feast restrain
A sudden thought of one so pale
    For love of her, and all in vain:

30   So, she was come through wind and rain.
     Be sure I looked up at her eyes
         Happy and proud; at last I knew
     Porphyria worshipped me: surprise
         Made my heart swell, and still it grew
35   While I debated what to do.
     That moment she was mine, mine, fair,
         Perfectly pure and good: I found
     A thing to do, and all her hair
         In one long yellow string I wound
40   Three times her little throat around,
     And strangled her. No pain felt she;
         I am quite sure she felt no pain.
     As a shut bud that holds a bee,
         I warily oped her lids: again
45   Laughed the blue eyes without a stain.
     And I untightened next the tress
         About her neck; her cheek once more
     Blushed bright beneath my burning kiss:
         I propped her head up as before,
50   Only, this time my shoulder bore
     Her head, which droops upon it still:
         The smiling rosy little head,
     So glad it has its utmost will,
         That all it scorned at once is fled,
55   And I, its love, am gained instead!
     Porphyria's love: she guessed not how
         Her darling one wish would be heard.
     And thus we sit together now,
         And all night long we have not stirred,
60   And yet God has not said a word!

This poem is about...

a woman, Porphyria, who visits her lover; he wants her to live with him but she won't so he strangles her and keeps her by his side.

How do lines 1–15 present Porphyria and her lover?

The title's reference to Porphyria's 'lover' implies that she is already married to someone else.

Pathetic fallacy suggests the speaker's depressed and **manic** state: the wind is described as miserable ('sullen') and violent ('tore the elm-tops down for spite'). When he says 'The rain set early in to-night', it could imply these feelings come to him every night. The idea of mental disturbance is also conveyed through how the wind 'did its worst to **vex** the lake', with the image of the unsettled water suggesting a loss of purity. The fifth line adds 'I listened with heart fit to break', suggesting that his madness is linked to his love for Porphyria.

Porphyria is shown through the speaker's unreliable perspective: we are unsure whether his version of events is real or partly fantasy. The verb 'glided' makes her sound magical and she is linked to images of heat: 'shut the cold out [...] made the cheerless grate / Blaze up, and all the cottage warm'. This could symbolise the speaker's passion, and the personification of the grate shows the uplifting effect that she has on him.

When the poem was written, it was improper for a woman to wear her hair down, so 'let the damp hair fall' is an erotic image of intimacy. The list of her removing her outer clothes builds up a sense of the speaker's obsession and passion. This is emphasised by how she 'called' him, with the verb suggesting he is almost in a trance and needs to be awoken.

How do lines 16–25 explore the relationship between the speaker and Porphyria?

Images of intimacy, 'put my arm about her waist, / And made her smooth white shoulder bare', and anaphora of 'And' build up a portrait of Porphyria's active **sensuality** and the speaker's obsession. This is emphasised by the repetition of her 'yellow hair'.

The poem suggests that, although she loves him ('Murmuring how she loved me'), Porphyria will not live with him because she is married or because he is below her social position: 'Too weak [...] / To set its struggling passion free / From pride, and vainer ties dissever, / And give herself to me for ever'. The noun 'pride' and the adjective 'vainer' could be Porphyria admitting her faults or the speaker criticising her reasons. The verb phrase 'give herself to me' reinforces the speaker's obsession.

How do lines 26–37 explore the speaker's obsession with Porphyria?

Her inability to resist him ('passion sometimes would prevail') is emphasised by alliteration. The speaker's love is described as a sickness, 'pale / For love of her', which links back to his feelings at the start of the poem and also relates to her name: porphyria is a disease, implying the speaker resents how she makes him feel. The speaker may also suffer from porphyria, which can cause anxiety and psychosis, perhaps explaining his behaviour in the poem.

The phrase 'Be sure' suggests the speaker is trying to convince either the audience or himself as he explains his realisation that 'Porphyria worshipped me'. The verb seems more appropriate to how he views her and when he sees her eyes are 'Happy and proud' there is another suggestion that she hasn't wanted to live with him because he is below her social status. The metaphor 'Made my heart swell' shows his joy and this is heightened by the verb phrase 'and still it grew'. The dreamlike mood created by the verbs and metaphors in this line suggests this is part of the speaker's fantasy rather than reality.

His happiness is contrasted with apparent anxiety: 'I debated what to do'. He doesn't want to lose this moment, describing it as 'she was mine, mine, fair, / Perfectly pure and good'; the tricolon of adjectives shows his **idealised** view of her while the repetition of the possessive pronoun reinforces his obsessive nature.

How is the murder presented on lines 37–41?

The speaker murders her using her hair, 'In one long yellow string', which was previously used as a symbol of eroticism. Turning it into a murder weapon suggests the speaker is killing what he loves, or could link back to the idea that he somehow blames her attractiveness for how it makes him feel.

The long vowels sounds in 'I wound / Three times her little throat around' slow the pace of the sentence to suggest the deliberate and strangely careful way in which he kills her, which is further emphasised by the rhyme. This contrasts with the bluntness of 'And strangled her', using caesura to pause the narrative mid-line and dwell on the murder. When he adds 'No pain felt she; / I am quite sure she felt no pain', the repetition adds a tone of doubt; the lines sound once again like he is trying to convince the reader or perhaps himself. The lines also appear to act as a disturbing defence of his actions.

At the end of the poem, how does the speaker respond to what he has done?

The speaker behaves as if Porphyria is alive. Metaphors describe how she looks happy, 'Laughed the blue eyes without a stain', and full of energy, 'her cheek once more / Blushed bright beneath my burning kiss'. The kiss metaphor shows his passion and alliterated plosives add a tone of aggression. The use of traditional romantic imagery (the flower simile, 'As a shut bud that holds a bee') makes the atmosphere even more disturbing, suggesting **necrophilia**.

He behaves as if nothing has happened, 'propped her head up as before', and presents signs that she is dead as if they are signs of her love: 'my shoulder bore / Her head, which droops upon it still'. He even suggests Porphyria is pleased: 'So glad it has its utmost will, / That all it scorned at once is fled, / And I, its love, am gained instead!' The adjective 'glad' and the abstract noun 'will' imply this is what she wanted; the verbs 'fled' and 'gained' suggest he has helped her escape her problems and given her a better life. The repetition of the impersonal pronoun 'it' relates to how he **objectifies** and arranges her body like a possession. His excitement is shown in the exclamation mark and he almost jokes about the murder: 'she guessed not how / Her darling one wish would be heard'.

The last two lines suggest he genuinely thinks God should praise him or he is taking God's silence as justification. It is the first time a plural pronoun ('we') is used, showing he finally considers he and Porphyria to be together.

How does the poem's form contribute to the way meaning is conveyed?

This is a dramatic monologue written in iambic tetrameter with an *ababb* rhyme scheme. The uniformity suggests the speaker is in control (perhaps linking to his obsessive nature) but the lack of stanzas creates continual, unbroken speech that could reflect his manic state. The poem also contains a lot of enjambment and caesura, regularly interrupting the rhythm to portray the underlying lack of control that, presumably, he hid from Porphyria until he killed her.

Lines 22 and 24–25 diverge from the rhythm slightly, with their final iambs replaced by amphibrachs. These lines give the reasons why she will not live with him so the change in rhythm may be highlighting the cause of his madness; the rhythmic fall created by the extra unstressed beat could also foreshadow how these reasons will lead to her death.

Additional context to consider

The dramatic monologue only offers the narrator's perspective. As he is mentally disturbed, it is unclear what is fantasy and reality: Porphyria may not have even been his lover. We are also told very little about the narrator; for instance it could actually be a woman. The first-person voice allows the poet to emphasise the speaker's obsession.

The obstacles to love that are presented (class, codes of morality) link to the poem's 19th-century context.

Browning was a **Victorian** poet; during this period, people became fascinated by new research into madness and criminal psychology.

Poetic links

- A disturbing relationship in 'The Farmer's Bride'.
- Unreliable perspectives of relationships in 'Before You Were Mine'.
- Poetic voice in 'The Farmer's Bride' or 'Singh Song!'.

Sample analysis

'Porphyria's Lover' and 'Love's Philosophy' both present obstacles to love. Porphyria is described using the metaphor 'Too weak, for all her heart's endeavour, / To set its struggling passion free' to imply that something restricts her. The adjective 'weak' contrasts with the verb 'struggling' to suggest a powerful force – perhaps marriage or social expectations – stops her from being 'free'. The lines also suggest that this is partly her own choice, that she is **repressing** her feelings; however, because the dramatic monologue is from the lover's unreliable perspective, this may simply reflect his frustrations with her.

Similarly, Shelley's poem presents a woman held back by social expectations. When the speaker argues 'The winds of Heaven mix for ever', he appears to be trying to relieve her concerns. The nature imagery and the reference to religion suggest she sees (presumably pre-marital) sex as unnatural and unholy. Furthermore, the adverbial phrase 'for ever' implies that another obstacle to love is her suspicion that he may not be faithful.

Questions

QUICK TEST
1. What are our first impressions of Porphyria?
2. Why might the narrative be unreliable?
3. What aspect of Porphyria's appearance does the speaker keep repeating?
4. What does the speaker believe Porphyria would think about the murder?

EXAM PRACTICE
Using one or two of the highlighted quotations to learn, write a paragraph exploring how Browning presents obsession.

SONNET 29 – 'I THINK OF THEE!'
by Elizabeth Barrett Browning

I think of thee! – my thoughts do twine and bud
About thee, as wild vines, about a tree,
Put out broad leaves, and soon there's nought to see
Except the straggling green which hides the wood.

5 Yet, O my palm-tree, be it understood
I will not have my thoughts instead of thee
Who art dearer, better! Rather, instantly
Renew thy presence; as a strong tree should,
Rustle thy boughs and set thy trunk all bare,

10 And let these bands of greenery which insphere thee
Drop heavily down, – burst, shattered, everywhere!
Because, in this deep joy to see and hear thee
And breathe within thy shadow a new air,
I do not think of thee – I am too near thee.

This poem is about...

passionate romantic thoughts and the wish to be close to a lover.

How do the opening lines present love?

The opening, exclamative phrase 'I think of thee!' conveys her joy whenever she thinks about her lover. The subsequent caesura creates a passionate dramatic pause, as if the mere thought of him takes her breath away. The phrase also introduces **archaic** language (thee, thy, art), adding to the mood of romance by making it sound like a piece of **classical** literature.

Barrett Browning begins to establish an extended metaphor in which the speaker is a vine and her lover a tree. The tree suggests the speaker sees her lover as strong and dependable, while the vine presents her as weaker. The lines 'my thoughts do twine and bud / About thee, as wild vines, about a tree' suggest she cannot stop thinking about him. The verbs 'twine and bud' imply that each thought strengthens her love. The nature imagery has a sexual undertone, created by the image of a flower opening ('bud'), the adjective 'wild' and the description of the vine spreading all over him.

The speaker's thoughts are presented as totally focused on her lover, taking over everything else. This is shown at the start of the phrase 'Put out broad leaves, and soon there's nought to see / Except the straggling green which hides the wood'. At the same time, the second part of this metaphor shows a desire to take over her lover's life until they become one entity rather than separate individuals.

How do lines 5–11 explore love further?

The sonnet develops from describing her thoughts about him to describing how she wants his physical presence.

The speaker addresses her lover with a similarly passionate exclamative phrase to line 1, 'O my palm-tree'. Palms have a religious **connotation** (Palm Sunday), suggesting she sees their love as spiritual. Although she thinks of him constantly, she would rather have him with her: 'I will not have my thoughts instead of thee / Who art dearer, better!' The comparative adjectives emphasise the strength of her feelings and these lines combine with line 5 to suggest their love is whole: physical and spiritual.

Her desperation to be with him is shown in the imperative 'instantly / Renew thy presence'. The adverb adds to her passionate tone while the abstract noun 'presence' makes the lover seem majestic or godlike.

The speaker loves him for who he is and wants him to remain true to himself. The lines 'as a strong tree should, / Rustle thy boughs and set thy trunk all bare' show a desire for him to be masculine and take control of their relationship. The verb phrases in line 9 describe the tree shaking off the vines that have grown over it, contrasting with the opening where she seemed to be taking control. This could also suggest she wants the man he actually is, not just the impression she's created in his absence.

She appears to gain an erotic thrill from his strength, showing a desire to be dominated: 'And let these bands of greenery which insphere thee / Drop heavily down, – burst, shattered, everywhere!' The contrast between the verbs 'insphere' and 'drop' shows willingness to be the weaker half of the relationship, while the tricolon of broken images at the end of line 11 displays an excited tone (partly created by the short clauses and the preceding caesura). This doesn't have to be sensual; the image could simply represent her joy at him appearing for real, rather than her relying on her thoughts.

How does the end of the poem emphasise the speaker's feelings?

The conjunction 'Because' signals a change in the poem as the speaker explains her feelings. She focuses on his presence, using a tricolon of verbs ('to see and hear thee / And breathe within thy shadow') to convey her 'deep joy' at being close to him. The reference to his shadow could describe how close she is or it could create a more erotic image of them at night. She describes a 'new air', suggesting he has improved her life, almost as if he has brought her back to life.

The final line, 'I do not think of thee – I am too near thee', **subverts** the opening line to reinforce the idea that when he is with her she doesn't need to think about him. This could be a sensual suggestion that her thoughts can become actions, or just mean she's happy and content when he's around.

How does the poem's form contribute to the way meaning is conveyed?

The sonnet is a traditional form of love poetry.

The poem generally **conforms** to the traditional sonnet structure: 14 lines, written in iambic pentameter with a clear rhyme scheme. The brevity and uniformity of the sonnet help to focus and emphasise the emotions being conveyed.

However, perhaps linking to her outpouring of passion, not all the lines are contained within the sonnet structure. For example, line 7 replaces the opening iamb with an anapaest while line 14 changes the final iamb to an amphibrach.

Additional context to consider

The poem is from a collection of sonnets about Elizabeth Barrett Browning's husband. Because they were so personal, she called the collection 'Sonnets from the Portuguese' and published them as if they were translations of a foreign poet's work.

The first-person perspective, addressed to the lover, increases the intimacy of the poem.

Placed in its 19th-century context, the poem conforms to traditional gender roles by presenting the male as stronger than the female. However, it ignores social **convention** by presenting a woman who fully expresses her emotions and desires.

Poetic links

- Romantic love in 'Love's Philosophy', 'Winter Swans' or 'Singh Song!'.
- Intimacy in 'Winter Swans' or 'Singh Song!'.
- Relationships and thoughts in 'Before You Were Mine', 'Walking Away', 'Eden Rock' or 'Climbing My Grandfather'.
- Nature imagery in 'Love's Philosophy', 'Neutral Tones', 'The Farmer's Bride', 'Winter Swans' or 'Climbing My Grandfather'.
- The use of extended metaphor in 'Love's Philosophy', 'Mother, any distance' or 'Climbing My Grandfather'.

Sample analysis

'I think of thee!' and 'Winter Swans' both use nature imagery to present relationships. Barrett Browning uses the extended metaphor of a vine and tree, 'Put out broad leaves, and soon there's nought to see / Except the straggling green which hides the wood', to present the idea that the speaker wants she and her lover to become like one person. The phrases 'nought to see' and 'hides' create an image of them getting happily lost in each other's life. The 'broad leaves' represent her thoughts about him and how these will take over all her other thoughts.

Sheers also uses nature imagery to present the unity of two lovers. The simile 'folded, one over the other, / like a pair of wings settling after flight' describes them holding hands after an argument. The verb 'folded' conveys closeness and security while 'wings' suggests mutual tenderness. The reference to 'flight' relates to the lovers' argument while the use of 'one', then 'other', then 'pair' depicts them reuniting.

Questions

QUICK TEST

1. Who is represented by the vine and who is represented by the tree?
2. What does the palm tree metaphor suggest?
3. What does the speaker want instead of her thoughts?
4. What does the phrase 'new air' suggest?

EXAM PRACTICE

Using one or two of the highlighted quotations to learn, write a paragraph exploring how Barrett Browning presents love.

We stood by a pond that winter day,
And the sun was white, as though chidden of God,
And a few leaves lay on the starving sod;
   – They had fallen from an ash, and were grey.

5   Your eyes on me were as eyes that rove
Over tedious riddles of years ago;
And some words played between us to and fro
   On which lost the more by our love.

The smile on your mouth was the deadest thing
10   Alive enough to have strength to die;
And a grin of bitterness swept thereby
   Like an ominous bird a-wing...

Since then, keen lessons that love deceives,
And wrings with wrong, have shaped to me
15   Your face, and the God curst sun, and a tree,
   And a pond edged with greyish leaves.

This poem is about...

looking back on the end of a relationship but feeling almost no emotion.

How is the neutral tone established in the first stanza?

The depiction of a relationship coming to an end brings a feeling of melancholy to the poem but there are no heightened emotions. Instead, the speaker's feelings appear deadened and this is presented through pathetic fallacy.

The opening line contains little description, 'We stood by a pond that winter day', conveying a blunt, matter-of-fact attitude to the end of their relationship. The reference to winter suggests a cold lack of emotion (between the couple then and from the speaker now). The setting seems strangely peaceful and the sibilance running through the stanza adds a hushed but sinister tone. The pond could symbolise emotional clarity as well as how their relationship can go no further; this point between land and water represents a boundary that has been reached.

The speaker's neutral emotions are reflected in Hardy's use of colour: the sun is 'white' and the leaves are 'grey'. The sun is referred to as 'chidden by God', with the verb (meaning told off or harshly criticised) suggesting all warmth has retreated, linking to the weather and the couple's lack of emotional warmth. Love is often linked to nature but, here, the 'fallen' leaves show love dying. Similarly, personification of the ground, 'starving sod', suggests that their relationship hasn't been looked after. Even the type of tree, 'ash', has connotations of death and coldness.

How does the second stanza present the relationship?

The poet presents a lack of communication and trust between the couple. The speaker describes how 'Your eyes on me were as eyes that rove / Over tedious riddles of years ago', revealing how they are both watching each other. The phrase suggests both are thinking about petty arguments that were never resolved ('tedious riddles'), while the phrase 'years ago' shows this is a long-term relationship coming to an end.

Their poor communication is reiterated, 'And some words played between us to and fro / On which lost the more by our love', with the verb 'played' suggesting they never try to seriously examine and solve what is wrong. The phrase 'to and fro' implies they never progress beyond their little arguments and they seem to resent each other (arguing who gave, and lost, 'more' to the relationship).

How is the speaker's lover presented in the third stanza?

The lack of honesty and emotion between the couple is demonstrated in the line 'The smile on your mouth was the deadest thing'. The contrast between the noun smile and the superlative adjective 'deadest' depicts how bad their relationship has become. The use of 'thing' suggests a lack of life but also a sense of repulsion.

The enjambment allows the sentence to run on and emphasise the worsening of the situation, 'Alive enough to have strength to die', retelling how even the dead smile fades from the lover's face. This image of something already dead then dying emphasises how appalling their relationship is but conveys it in the poem's same emotionless manner.

Emotions turned sour are also shown in the simile 'grin of bitterness swept thereby / Like an **ominous** bird a-wing…', with the ellipsis and the adjective 'ominous' suggesting worse was to come.

How has the speaker been affected by the relationship?

The fact he is looking back ('Since then') suggests the experience still affects him. Personification perhaps explains his cold behaviour when he states 'love deceives'.

The metaphor 'keen lessons' suggests the relationship was a sharply painful mistake while alliteration emphasises his belief he was unfairly hurt: 'wrings with wrong'. It also suggests that he is thinking of other failed relationships that remind him of this experience.

He summarises the relationship with little feeling ('Your face, and the God curst sun, and a tree, / And a pond edged with greyish leaves'), adding the adjective phrase 'God curst' to suggest it was doomed from the beginning.

How does the poem's form contribute to the way meaning is conveyed?

The poem is arranged in four quatrains with an *abba* rhyme scheme that could reflect the couple's fractured relationship.

Although they don't follow a uniform rhythm, the first three lines of each stanza are always written in tetrameter (carrying four stressed beats) and the last lines in trimeter (with three stressed beats). This creates a weakness at the end of each stanza that reflects the weakness at the end of the couple's relationship. The lines also contain anapaests to add a higher proportion of unstressed beats and convey the speaker's **despondent** tone:

and a FEW leaves LAY on the STARving SOD

the SMILE on your MOUTH was the DEADest THING

The poem is also structured in a circular (rather than **linear**) way, starting and ending at the pond, to show the speaker's thoughts and feelings are unresolved.

Additional context to consider

The use of the past tense emphasises the idea of a relationship being over but addressing the poem to the speaker's ex-lover shows the long-term effect of the relationship (because the lover is still on the speaker's mind).

The lack of gender allows the reader to relate the poem to a variety of relationships, just as the lack of specific description (and use of indefinite articles, 'a tree […] a pond') makes the poem more universal.

Poetic links

- Lack of love in 'When We Two Parted', 'Love's Philosophy' or 'The Farmer's Bride'.
- The end of a relationship in 'When We Two Parted'.
- A problem in a relationship in 'Love's Philosophy', 'The Farmer's Bride' or 'Winter Swans'.
- Nature imagery in 'Love's Philosophy', 'I think of thee!', 'The Farmer's Bride', 'Winter Swans' or 'Climbing My Grandfather'.

Sample analysis

Whereas 'Neutral Tones' presents separation, 'I think of thee!' presents intimacy. Hardy's lines 'Your eyes on me were as eyes that rove / Over tedious riddles of years ago' present a lack of trust and unity. The speaker's focus on the lover's eyes suggests they are both watching each other, which implies mutual suspicion, while the phrase 'tedious riddles' indicates small arguments that are repeated and never resolved. Placing the poem in the past tense and looking back to 'years ago' emphasises the idea of separation.

In contrast, Barrett Browning presents an intimate relationship in the present tense. The lines 'in this deep joy to see and hear thee / And breathe within thy shadow a new air' convey physical closeness by the speaker standing in her lover's shadow. This could also be interpreted as a sensual description of them together at night. The tricolon of verbs suggests she feels alive when close to him and this is emphasised by the image of 'new air'. Barrett Browning summarises the happiness of intimacy in the noun phrase 'deep joy', contrasting with the 'tedious riddles' of Hardy's poem.

Questions

QUICK TEST

1. How does Hardy use pathetic fallacy in the first stanza?
2. What problem is presented in the second stanza?
3. What lesson does the speaker learn about love?
4. How are the poet's language choices 'neutral'?

EXAM PRACTICE

Using one or two of the highlighted quotations to learn, write a paragraph exploring how Hardy presents the end of a relationship.

LETTERS FROM YORKSHIRE
by Maura Dooley

In February, digging his garden, planting potatoes,
he saw the first lapwings return and came
indoors to write to me, his knuckles singing

as they reddened in the warmth.
5   It's not romance, simply how things are.
You out there, in the cold, seeing the seasons

turning, me with my heartful of headlines
feeding words onto a blank screen.
Is your life more real because you dig and sow?

10   You wouldn't say so, breaking ice on a waterbutt,
clearing a path through snow. Still, it's you
who sends me word of that other world

pouring air and light into an envelope. So that
at night, watching the same news in different houses,
15   our souls tap out messages across the icy miles.

This poem is about...

a platonic long-distance relationship.

How do the first four lines present the speaker's friend?

The opening line uses verbs to show the man is active, 'In February, digging his garden, planting potatoes', with plosives reflecting physical exertion. He is presented as having a peaceful, **rural** life and being interested in nature: 'saw the first lapwings return'.

It implies that he 'came / indoors' immediately, showing he is eager to share the highlights of his life and suggesting the speaker has a mutual interest in nature. The internal rhyme of 'he' and 'me' in lines 2–3 represents both their similarity and their geographical distance.

The metaphor 'his knuckles singing / as they reddened in the warmth' suggests he is a hardy man as he isn't concerned by the pain (from his nerves reacting to the sudden change in temperature). 'Singing' also emphasises his eagerness to write straight away, rather than waiting for his hands to warm up properly, by suggesting joy and pain simultaneously. This description implies the speaker is imagining the man's feelings, showing concern and suggesting familiarity with the way he behaves.

How do lines 5–8 present the relationship?

The speaker states 'It's not romance, simply how things are', indicating that people have an idealised view of country life but, to the man, it's just normality. The line also implies the speaker is a woman and so her friendship with the man is sometimes misread by others as a romantic relationship. The adverb 'simply' suggests the relationship carries no complex baggage or emotions; they are just friends who keep in touch. This is emphasised by the short sentence and how the caesura separates and highlights each clause.

The speaker uses a contrast to suggest their friendship seems unlikely because they live such different lives. The man's rural lifestyle is conveyed through outdoors images: 'You out there, in the cold, seeing the seasons / turning'. The speaker's indoors life is described through metaphor, 'my heartful of headlines / feeding words onto a blank screen', suggesting she is a journalist in a city. However, the poet's choice of words shows similarities between the two: 'heartful' could link to the man's pleasure at seeing the lapwings, while 'feeding' could relate to the way the man tends his garden. Their closeness is highlighted by the sudden switch to the second person ('You').

The juxtaposition of 'seasons' and 'headlines' suggests the man's pace of life is slower than the speaker's (as headlines link to daily change). The enjambment allows the pronouns 'you' and 'me' to be in the same sentence but different stanzas, representing their close friendship and its geographical distance.

How do lines 9–15 explore the relationship further?

The speaker poses a rhetorical question, 'Is your life more real because you dig and sow?', as she considers their different lifestyles. This could link back to line 8, with 'blank screen' perhaps being a metaphor for a life she sees as empty because it's too focused on work.

Their friendship is shown by her understanding that he doesn't dismiss her way of life: 'You wouldn't say so, breaking ice on a waterbutt, / clearing a path through snow'. The verb phrases (breaking ice, clearing a path) show her awareness that his life has its difficulties, although they could also symbolise freedom and clarity to suggest she envies his lifestyle.

This is emphasised by the lines 'it's you / who sends me word of that other world / pouring air and light into an envelope', using metaphor to suggest how much joy she gets from reading his letters. The use of 'air' and 'light' conveys the idea that reading his letters is like being there in Yorkshire with him. The phrase 'other world' suggests his lifestyle is almost a dream that she could never attain.

The poem ends with several images of intimacy and distance. The line 'at night, watching the same news in different houses' suggests individual loneliness that is soothed by their friendship. The contrasting adjectives 'same' and 'different' summarise their friendship, while the reference to 'news' highlights shared concerns as people living in the same country.

This is followed by the metaphor 'our souls tap out messages across the icy miles', implying that they **subconsciously** know each is thinking of the other, with the alliteration connecting the words that link to closeness ('messages') and distance ('miles'). Significantly, the singular pronouns (he, his, you, me, my) that are used throughout the poem finally give way to a comforting plural pronoun: 'our'.

How does the poem's form contribute to the way meaning is conveyed?

The poem is arranged in five tercets in free verse. This mix of uniformity and variation could reflect the idea that the friends share a common link but live completely different lives. Many of the lines also use enjambment, perhaps reflecting a friendship that continues despite geographical distance.

The lack of fixed structure helps the poem to mirror ordinary speech, strengthening its depiction of two friends.

Additional context to consider

The language in the poem is straightforward, mirroring an informal relationship but also allowing the poem to relate to a variety of people and situations. The lack of specific details (such as age, the speaker's gender, their actual relationship) adds to its broader reach.

Poetic links

- A separated relationship in 'When We Two Parted', 'Walking Away' or 'Eden Rock'.
- Different types of people in a relationship in 'Mother, any distance' or 'The Farmer's Bride'.

Sample analysis

'Letters from Yorkshire' and 'Neutral Tones' present different types of distance in a relationship. Dooley presents close friends who are geographically separated, 'that other world / pouring air and light into an envelope', using a metaphor to show how the woman can imagine being in the same place as the man when she reads his letters. The references to 'air' and light' suggest how their friendship enriches her life even though they are miles apart. This distance is emphasised by using hyperbole to describe Yorkshire as 'that other world', followed by enjambment to separate it from the remainder of the sentence.

In contrast, Hardy presents a couple who are physically close but emotionally distant. The opening line, 'We stood by a pond that winter day', uses pathetic fallacy to convey their lack of feeling for each other despite their closeness (represented by the plural pronoun 'we'). Placing them at a boundary between land and water also symbolises the end point of their relationship and this is emphasised by Hardy's use of the past tense in comparison to Dooley's present tense.

Questions

QUICK TEST

1. How does the man's life seem different to the speaker's?
2. What does the speaker clearly state about the relationship?
3. What images are used to show their close friendship?
4. How does the enjambment link to the meaning of the poem?

EXAM PRACTICE

Using one or two of the highlighted quotations to learn, write a paragraph exploring how Dooley presents closeness and distance.

THE FARMER'S BRIDE
by Charlotte Mew

Three Summers since I chose a maid,
Too young maybe – but more's to do
At harvest-time than bide and woo.
    When us was wed she turned afraid
5 Of love and me and all things human;
Like the shut of a winter's day
Her smile went out, and 'twasn't a woman –
    More like a little frightened fay.
        One night, in the Fall, she runned away.

10 'Out 'mong the sheep, her be,' they said,
Should properly have been abed;
But sure enough she wasn't there
Lying awake with her wide brown stare.
    So over seven-acre field and up-along across the down
15 We chased her, flying like a hare
Before our lanterns. To Church-Town
    All in a shiver and a scare
We caught her, fetched her home at last
    And turned the key upon her, fast.

20 She does the work about the house
As well as most, but like a mouse:
    Happy enough to chat and play
    With birds and rabbits and such as they,
    So long as men-folk keep away.
25 'Not near, not near!' her eyes beseech
When one of us comes within reach.

The women say that beasts in stall
Look round like children at her call.
I've hardly heard her speak at all.

30 Shy as a leveret, swift as he,
Straight and slight as a young larch tree,
Sweet as the first wild violets, she,
To her wild self. But what to me?

The short days shorten and the oaks are brown,
35   The blue smoke rises to the low grey sky,
One leaf in the still air falls slowly down,
    A magpie's spotted feathers lie
On the black earth spread white with rime,
The berries redden up to Christmas-time.
40   What's Christmas-time without there be
Some other in the house than we!

She sleeps up in the attic there
Alone, poor maid. 'Tis but a stair
Betwixt us. Oh! my God! the down,
45 The soft young down of her, the brown,
The brown of her – her eyes, her hair, her hair!

This poem is about...

a young girl whose family marry her to an older farmer; she is terrified by his sexual advances.

How does the first stanza present the relationship?

We are told the marriage took place 'Three Summers' ago and it is presented as a business transaction rather than a romance. The farmer says he 'chose a maid' and the verb implies she had no choice and there was no **courtship** (in order to improve their own financial status, poor families sometimes married their girls off to wealthier men). This is reinforced when he says he was too busy to '**woo**'. He wonders if she was 'Too young maybe', a small sign of his regret that is emphasised by the subsequent caesura.

The farmer establishes the problem in their relationship through a tricolon: 'When us was wed she turned afraid / Of love and me and all things human'. The last phrase is a reference to sex, showing that the young girl was terrified. Similes are used to show her unhappiness, 'Like the shut of a winter's day / Her smile went out', and her nervous, timid behaviour: 'like a little frightened **fay**'. The way she is described suggests the farmer forced himself upon her and she is traumatised.

How is sympathy for the bride built up in stanza 2?

When the farmer says she 'Should properly have been abed', the adverb shows that he sees it as his wife's duty to sleep with him. It is clear that she shared his bed many times even though she was terrified, 'Lying awake with her wide brown stare'.

When she runs away, her pursuit is described like a hunt: 'over seven-acre field and up-along across the down / We chased her'. The contrast of plural and singular pronouns heightens the sense of her vulnerability and this is also shown in the simile 'flying like a hare'. The animal imagery reinforces how, because she is poor and female, she has been treated as less than human. The reference to 'Church-Town' could be a criticism of how marriages like hers were allowed to take place.

The men are aware of, but unsympathetic to, her fear ('All in a shiver and a scare'). Verbs are used to show how she is treated like one of the farmer's animals or belongings: 'We caught her, fetched her home'. The way in which she is valuable to the farmer, despite him not actually valuing her, is shown in the way she is locked up: 'turned the key upon her, fast'.

How do the third and fourth stanzas present the marriage?

The farmer admits the bride fulfils what he sees as her domestic duties: 'does the work about the house / As well as most'. She is described as comfortable around animals, 'Happy enough to chat and play / With birds and rabbits', with the verbs reflecting her youth and innocence. In contrast, she is terrified of men: '"Not near, not near!" her eyes **beseech** / When one of us comes within reach'. Repetition emphasises her terror, as does the verb 'beseech'; the rhyming with 'reach' highlights her fear of being sexually assaulted.

Similes compare her to nature to reiterate her youth, innocence and vulnerability: 'like a mouse', 'Shy as a leveret' (a young hare), 'slight as a young larch tree', 'Sweet as the first wild violets'. These descriptions also increasingly show the farmer's lust by focusing on her body or scent. His comment '*I've hardly heard her speak at all*', and the rhetorical question 'But what to me?', show he desires her and doesn't understand her behaviour.

How do the last two stanzas show the farmer's feelings about the marriage?

The farmer describes winter in a peaceful way, perhaps suggesting a gentler side of his character that he never knew how to show his bride. He reveals he wants children, 'What's Christmas-time without there be / Some other in the house than we!', and the references to winter ('The short days shorten') could indicate he worries he's getting too old to have them.

He displays regret or guilt for his treatment of his bride: 'Alone, poor maid'. This is contrasted with his sexual frustration: ''Tis but a stair / **Betwixt** us. Oh! my God! the down, / The soft young down of her, the brown, / The brown of her – her eyes, her hair, her hair!' The adjectives to describe her body, plus the repetition and exclamations within short clauses that are full of pauses for breath, present his desire and could depict him as masturbating while he lies in the bedroom below her.

How does the poem's form contribute to the way meaning is conveyed?

This dramatic monologue is generally written in iambic tetrameter but several lines in each stanza don't match this metre. Similarly, there are lots of rhymes (especially rhyming couplets) but no set pattern and the stanzas are of different lengths. The aspects of uniformity could reflect the farmer's expectations of a traditional marriage, while the unstructured elements could link to how he can't fit his bride into this marital framework. Not strictly following a metre or rhyme scheme also adds more realism to the narrative voice.

 Additional context to consider

The poem is best understood through its context as it is set in the countryside in the past. This explains the attitudes to marriage, the dominance of men and the fact no one appears to try to help the girl, the bride's lack of understanding of sex (she wouldn't have received sex education), the farmer's sexist attitudes and his need for a son to inherit his land, and neither husband nor wife understanding the opposite sex.

The farmer's narrative voice allows sympathy for both him and his bride. His background and job are partly presented through non-standard English, such as dialect (''twasn't') and incorrect grammar ('runned away'). The farmer's job is also reflected in the amount of animal imagery used, suggesting it's all he knows about in life.

Poetic links

- A disturbing relationship in 'Porphyria's Lover'.
- Lack of love in 'When We Two Parted', 'Love's Philosophy' or 'Neutral Tones'.
- A problem in a relationship in 'Love's Philosophy', 'Neutral Tones' or 'Winter Swans'.
- Desire in 'Love's Philosophy' or 'Singh Song!'.
- Poetic voice in 'Porphyria's Lover' and 'Singh Song!'.
- Marriage in 'Singh Song!'.
- Nature imagery in 'Love's Philosophy', 'I think of thee!', 'Neutral Tones', 'Winter Swans' or 'Climbing My Grandfather'.

Sample analysis

'The Farmer's Bride' and 'Porphyria's Lover' present disturbing relationships. Imagining the farmer may only have been taught to farm, Mew uses animal imagery to show he doesn't understand or properly value women. The simile 'We chased her, flying like a hare' depicts the bride's attempt to escape their marriage, and the verb 'chased' suggests it's like a hunt that the farmer enjoys. The contrast of plural and singular pronouns emphasises her vulnerability and implies that she feels outnumbered and in danger on the farm.

Browning also uses a dramatic monologue to present a speaker's disturbing relationship with a woman. After killing her, he arranges her body – 'I propped her head up as before, / [...] The smiling rosy little head' – and 'smiling' implies he thinks she is happy. The adjectives suggest that he does actually love her, linking to the portrayal of the speaker as deluded and insane. Like 'chased' in 'The Farmer's Bride', the verb 'propped' is used to convey the speaker's desire to dominate and control.

Questions

QUICK TEST

1. How does Mew imply the bride's lack of choice?
2. What doesn't the farmer seem to understand?
3. What animals are the bride compared to?
4. What does the farmer want at the end of the poem?

EXAM PRACTICE

Using one or two of the highlighted quotations to learn, write a paragraph exploring how Mew shows the farmer's attitude to his bride.

WALKING AWAY by Cecil Day Lewis

It is eighteen years ago, almost to the day –
A sunny day with leaves just turning,
The touch-lines new-ruled – since I watched you play
Your first game of football, then, like a satellite
5 Wrenched from its orbit, go drifting away

Behind a scatter of boys. I can see
You walking away from me towards the school
With the pathos of a half-fledged thing set free
Into a wilderness, the gait of one
10 Who finds no path where the path should be.

That hesitant figure, eddying away
Like a winged seed loosened from its parent stem,
Has something I never quite grasp to convey
About nature's give-and-take – the small, the scorching
15 Ordeals which fire one's irresolute clay.

I have had worse partings, but none that so
Gnaws at my mind still. Perhaps it is roughly
Saying what God alone could perfectly show –
How selfhood begins with a walking away,
20 And love is proved in the letting go.

This poem is about...

a parental relationship as a father watches his son grow up and move away from him.

How does the first stanza present the father's feelings?

The speaker recalls the first time he realised his son would move away from him: 'It is eighteen years ago, almost to the day'.

The poet uses a series of images related to change. The first links to nature, 'A sunny day with leaves just turning', to show change is natural and inevitable, with the autumnal reference ('turning') a metaphor for the son growing up. The image incorporates pathetic fallacy: the sun represents the father's happiness, while the leaves foreshadow the sadness to come. The son is about to play his 'first game of football', an experience that can never be repeated. Furthermore, the speaker describes the pitch's 'touch-lines new-ruled', but this will have changed by the end of the match; touch lines are white, which could also symbolise the boy's innocence.

A simile conveys the speaker's awareness that he will lose his son: 'like a satellite / Wrenched from its orbit, go drifting away'. The 'satellite' suggests something smaller, almost dependent, and contrasting verbs (the forceful 'wrenched' and the gentler 'drifting') show the father's pain while implying the son will be oblivious. The inability to hold on to his son is emphasised by the enjambment, making the sentence run on rather than stop. A verb phrase including the word 'away' appears in each stanza (lines 5, 7, 11 and 19).

How is the son presented in the second stanza?

The phrase 'Behind a scatter of boys' acknowledges that all children move on. The speaker thinks of his son's first day at a new school, 'You walking away from me towards the school', and the poet symbolically uses the verb phrase to separate the two pronouns. The school could represent a loss of innocence and might also suggest irony in the way parents prepare their children for independence but, at the same time, don't want to let go of them.

The son's reluctance to be parted from his father is described as 'the **pathos** of a half-**fledged** thing set free / Into a wilderness'. He felt sorry for his son, feeling he wasn't yet ready ('half-fledged') to be independent. The idea that this situation is both unavoidable and scary is conveyed through enjambment, continuing the sentence without a pause while highlighting the switch from the positive connotations of 'free' to the negative connotations of 'wilderness'. The boy's uncertainty and wish for his father's guidance is shown in 'one / Who finds no path where the path should be'.

How do the last two stanzas explore the separation of a parent and child?

The speaker continues presenting his son as gradually moving away from him with the simile 'That hesitant figure, eddying away / Like a winged seed loosened from its parent stem'. Nature imagery is used again to show this is a natural process, using the comparison to a seed to indicate a child needs to be independent in order to properly grow. The adjective 'hesitant' repeats the son's uncertainty and the father's sadness while the verb 'eddying' refers to the wind to suggest that growing up isn't always a smooth process and it can't be stopped either.

The speaker describes 'nature's give-and-take – the small, the scorching / Ordeals which fire one's irresolute clay', accepting the way parents look after children only for them to move away. The clay-baking metaphor conveys how the early painful experiences of a child's 'small' steps towards independence (depicted in this poem through the football match and the first day at a new school) prepare the parent for when they finally separate. The adjective 'irresolute' highlights how parents never want this day of separation to come. The speaker acknowledges 'worse partings' but says his son's parting 'Gnaws at my mind still', using a metaphor to suggest constant pain.

The final lines, 'How selfhood begins with a walking away, / And love is proved in the letting go', show the necessity for a child to grow up and move away in order to become his or her own person. This is followed by the idea that parents show their strongest love by accepting that the child needs to move away. The verb phrases at the end of each line imply a decisive action that needs to be taken by both parties. The idea that parents have to be selfless and accept the pain caused by their children leaving is linked to sacrifice by an allusion to the biblical story of God sacrificing his son, Jesus: 'Saying what God alone could perfectly show'.

How does the poem's form contribute to the way meaning is conveyed?

This is an autobiographical, lyric poem addressed from father to son. It is arranged in four quintets and written in free verse but with an *abaca* rhyme scheme.

The combination of structure (stanzas of a uniform length and a regular rhyme scheme) and lack of structure (not using a fixed metre) could reflect the way parenting is described in the poem: care and guidance taking place simultaneously with the gradual giving of freedom and independence.

Additional context to consider

Although the poem is autobiographical, a parent's response to their child moving away from home is a universal experience. The poem maintains this by avoiding specific proper nouns, describing familiar situations and using free verse to partially mirror natural speech.

The use of the father's first-person perspective intensifies the emotions in the poem, as does addressing it to the son.

Poetic links

- A separated relationship in 'When We Too Parted', 'Letters from Yorkshire' or 'Eden Rock'.
- Relationships and thoughts in 'I think of thee!', 'Eden Rock', 'Before You Were Mine' or 'Climbing My Grandfather'.
- Growing up in 'Mother, any distance' or 'Follower'.
- Family relationships in 'Eden Rock', 'Follower', 'Mother, any distance', 'Before You Were Mine' or 'Climbing My Grandfather'.

Sample analysis

'Walking Away' and 'Mother, any distance' explore how children grow up and move away from their parents. Day Lewis uses the metaphor 'the small, the scorching / Ordeals which fire one's irresolute clay' to present the parent's pain from giving a child increasing independence. The adjective 'scorching' suggests emotional scars (linking to how the poem features small memories), contrasting with the more positive connotations of the verb 'fire' to suggest the parent is eventually strong enough to part with their child.

Armitage explores a similar situation from a child's perspective, perhaps explaining why his images often link to exploration and uncertainty rather than pain and unhappiness. The parent is presented through the metaphors 'Anchor. Kite', conveying how parents offer stability but also restrict the child's freedom. Short sentences and plosive sounds emphasise the solid but oppressive nature of parenting, while the kite also represents the child's eagerness to escape and be free.

Questions

QUICK TEST

1. What similes present a child's gradual independence?
2. How does the poem show the father's anxieties about the child's independence?
3. What image shows that the parent is preparing to let his child go?
4. What act and emotion are linked to letting a child go?

EXAM PRACTICE

Using one or two of the highlighted quotations to learn, write a paragraph exploring how Day Lewis presents parental love.

EDEN ROCK by Charles Causley

They are waiting for me somewhere beyond Eden Rock:
My father, twenty-five, in the same suit
Of Genuine Irish Tweed, his terrier Jack
Still two years old and trembling at his feet.

5 My mother, twenty-three, in a sprigged dress
Drawn at the waist, ribbon in her straw hat,
Has spread the stiff white cloth over the grass.
Her hair, the colour of wheat, takes on the light.

She pours tea from a Thermos, the milk straight
10 From an old H.P. Sauce bottle, a screw
Of paper for a cork; slowly sets out
The same three plates, the tin cups painted blue.

The sky whitens as if lit by three suns.
My mother shades her eyes and looks my way
15 Over the drifted stream. My father spins
A stone along the water. Leisurely,

They beckon to me from the other bank.
I hear them call, 'See where the stream-path is!
Crossing is not as hard as you might think.'

20 I had not thought that it would be like this.

This poem is about...

the speaker's dead parents and his own feelings of **mortality**.

How is the speaker's father presented in the first stanza?

The opening line creates a strange setting. It is specific (the proper noun, Eden Rock) yet vague ('somewhere beyond') and can be seen as a presentation of the afterlife or a point between life and death. Eden contains connotations of paradise and God. The verb 'waiting' suggests the speaker expects to see his parents when he dies and perhaps thinks that will be soon.

The speaker describes a vision of his father from the past: 'My father, twenty-five, in the same suit / Of Genuine Irish Tweed'. However, 'twenty-five' implies this could be an image of a time before the speaker was born rather than an actual memory. The adjective 'same' suggests that, once he had been born, the speaker remembers regularly seeing his father wearing the suit. The specific reference to 'Genuine Irish Tweed' could suggest his father liked status or believed things should be done properly; it also indicates **thriftiness** as he wore it many times.

This vision of the past is added to with 'his terrier Jack / Still two years old and trembling at his feet'. The adverb 'still' shows the speaker has experienced the dog getting older, perhaps even dying. The verb 'trembling' could suggest the speaker's father is quite a dominant man.

How do the second and third stanzas present the speaker's mother?

The mother is described as 'twenty-three', again suggesting this could be an image from before the speaker was born rather than a memory. She is linked to traditional images of **femininity**: her dress is decorated with flowers ('sprigged') and shows off her figure ('Drawn at the waist'), and she is wearing a 'ribbon in her straw hat'. Her hair is also compared to nature, 'the colour of wheat, takes on the light', creating a dreamlike impression.

She is linked to **domesticity**: 'spread the stiff white cloth'. The adjective 'stiff' could reflect the traditional role of a housewife (that she seems happy to fulfil), while 'white' creates a sense of purity and perfection. The speaker describes how she 'pours tea [...] slowly sets out / The same three plates', reinforcing the image of a dutiful wife. The 'three' plates link back to the first line and suggest they are 'waiting' for him. She is also presented as thrifty: 'old H.P. Sauce bottle, a screw / Of paper for a cork [...] the tin cups'.

How does the second half of the poem explore mortality?

Like line 8, there is a dreamlike quality to line 13, 'The sky whitens as if lit by three suns', perhaps creating a vision of the light that people claim precedes the entry to the afterlife.

The speaker is presented as separated from his parents: 'looks my way / Over the drifted stream'. The distance is emphasised by the image of his father skimming 'A stone along the water'. The lack of actual communication adds to the dreamlike atmosphere and this is heightened by the way the enjambment of the adverb 'Leisurely' leaves the stanza hanging on an unhurried pause.

Communication then becomes more direct: 'They beckon to me from the other bank'. This suggests the speaker is aware of his own mortality and is imagining joining them in the afterlife; the verb 'beckon' suggests it is a good place. When he hears them call, 'See where the stream-path is! / Crossing is not as hard as you might think', there is an allusion to myths about crossing a river (like Lethe or Styx) to the afterlife. The adjective phrase 'not as hard' suggests that thoughts of his parents comfort him as he nears death.

The striking ending, 'I had not thought that it would be like this', is emphasised by it being a single-line stanza. The ominous reference to 'it' almost sounds as if the speaker is describing his actual moment of death as he moves towards the afterlife. The line captures the speaker's thoughts about dying but the tone is **ambiguous**: although the rest of the poem suggests a feeling of comfort, there is also a sense that something is wrong.

How does the poem's form contribute to the way meaning is conveyed?

This elegy is arranged in quatrains, although the final stanza is broken up to emphasise the final line. Most of the lines are written in iambic pentameter but there are exceptions, such as lines 15 and 19 where the opening iambs are substituted for trochees (CROSSing is NOT as HARD as YOU might THINK). There is a clear *abab* rhyme scheme but they are almost all half-rhymes (rock/Jack; suit/feet).

Causley appears to be deliberately structuring his poem in a way that makes it not seem quite right, perhaps reflecting the suggestion of uncertainty in the last line or mirroring the poem's overall dreamlike atmosphere with its visions of a past that the speaker may not have actually experienced.

Additional context to consider

The first-person perspective and the use of present tense add intimacy to the poem. However, to match the **abstract** subject matter, the poet is deliberately ambiguous. Very specific details about his parents (which might also seem familiar to the readers' lives) are combined with vague descriptions of the place to create an almost **surreal** atmosphere.

The poem is semi-autobiographical and this helps to unlock its meaning. Causley wrote the poem when he was in his seventies; his mother had died 17 years before while his father had died when Causley was only seven. His parents were in their early thirties when he was born, linking to the idea that the memories in the poem are idealised visions that Causley never actually experienced. He also places them in an imaginary setting as Eden Rock isn't a real place.

Poetic links

- A separated relationship in 'When We Too Parted', 'Letters from Yorkshire' or 'Walking Away'.
- Family relationships in 'Walking Away', 'Follower', 'Mother, any distance', 'Before You Were Mine' or 'Climbing My Grandfather'.
- Relationships and thoughts in 'I think of thee!', 'Walking Away', 'Before You Were Mine' or 'Climbing My Grandfather'.
- Memories in 'Follower'.

Sample analysis

'Eden Rock' and 'Walking Away' show strong family connections despite separation. Causley's poem suggests that the speaker imagines his parents calling him to the afterlife. The lines 'They beckon to me from the other bank. / [...] "Crossing is not as hard as you might think"' use the adjective phrase 'not as hard' to suggest thinking about his parents brings some comfort to the idea of dying. The verbs 'crossing' and, particularly, 'beckon' imply he looks forward to joining them while the half-rhymes that run throughout the poem help to create a suitably gentle tone by softening the line endings.

Day Lewis's poem presents a more familiar scenario of a father's love for a son who has moved away from home. The metaphor 'Gnaws at my mind still' shows he is always thinking of his son and their parting is a constant pain. However, the animal imagery also highlights the father's awareness that growing up and being independent is a natural part of all life in the world.

Questions

QUICK TEST
1. How does the first line create a strange setting?
2. Where is the mother linked to femininity and domesticity?
3. What phrases create a dreamlike atmosphere?
4. What do the speaker's parents appear to be doing at the end?

EXAM PRACTICE
Using one or two of the highlighted quotations to learn, write a paragraph exploring how Causley presents the speaker's feelings about his parents.

FOLLOWER by Seamus Heaney

My father worked with a horse-plough,
His shoulders globed like a full sail strung
Between the shafts and the furrow.
The horse strained at his clicking tongue.

5 An expert. He would set the wing
And fit the bright steel-pointed sock.
The sod rolled over without breaking.
At the headrig, with a single pluck

Of reins, the sweating team turned round
10 And back into the land. His eye
Narrowed and angled at the ground,
Mapping the furrow exactly.

I stumbled in his hob-nailed wake,
Fell sometimes on the polished sod;
15 Sometimes he rode me on his back
Dipping and rising to his plod.

I wanted to grow up and plough,
To close one eye, stiffen my arm.
All I ever did was follow
20 In his broad shadow round the farm.

I was a nuisance, tripping, falling,
Yapping always. But today
It is my father who keeps stumbling
Behind me, and will not go away.

This poem is about...

the changing relationship between a son and his father.

How does the first stanza present the speaker's father?

The opening line looks back on the past, indicated by the use of the past tense and the reference to an old-fashioned 'horse-plough' rather than a plough drawn by a modern tractor. The plough and the act of annual ploughing symbolise the idea of cycles and change; it can also link to the way the speaker is digging up his thoughts about his father.

The father is linked to hard work, first through the simple verb 'worked', then the more complex simile 'His shoulders globed like a full sail strung / Between the shafts and the furrow'. This conveys the strength needed to guide the horse and push the plough into the ground. The word 'globed' shows how the man's arms are wide and his muscles prominent, with the ship image suggesting he is using all his effort ('full sail').

The impressive image of his father is completed by showing he is in full command of the more powerful horse: 'The horse strained at his clicking tongue'. The contrast between the forceful verb 'strained' and the gentler noun phrase 'clicking tongue' emphasises the father's skill.

How do the second and third stanzas develop our impression of the speaker's father?

The second stanza opens with 'An expert'. The short sentence emphasises the compliment while reflecting his strength and also, perhaps, his simple way of life. His expertise is also conveyed through the practical verbs 'set' and 'fit' and the farming **jargon**: 'wing [...] sock [...] headrig'. The use of these words additionally shows how the speaker looked up to, and learned from, his father; his admiration is also evident in the adjective phrase 'bright steel-pointed' when describing the plough.

The speaker's respect for his father's skill is conveyed by how the ploughing was made to look easy: 'The sod rolled over without breaking. / [...] a single pluck / Of reins'. The enjambment represents his father's continuous, uninterrupted work and how the speaker marvels at his father's abilities.

He continues to describe his father as hardworking (the verb 'sweating') and skilful (the verbs 'narrowed', 'angled' and 'mapping', and the adverb 'exactly'). However, an undertone of discontent can be inferred in the speaker's words at this point: he refers to father and horse as a 'team', perhaps indicating he feels left out; he describes his father's 'eye [...] at the ground', suggesting he receives no attention.

How do the fourth and fifth stanzas depict the speaker's relationship with his father?

The verbs 'stumbled' and 'fell' describe the speaker's clumsiness. The phrase 'in his hob-nailed wake' suggests he is always following his father but never catching up, linking to the poem's title.

The speaker describes moments of intimacy when he 'rode me on his back / Dipping and rising to his plod'. However, 'to his plod' depicts the speaker's feeling that he is still just following rather than being independent. The image is also childish, leading to the admission 'I wanted to grow up'.

The speaker wanted to match his father, 'plough, / To close one eye, stiffen my arm', with the verbs indicating the same skill and strength depicted in stanza 1. He describes his failure: 'All I ever did was follow / In his broad shadow round the farm'. The verb 'follow' emphasises the poem's central idea while the metaphor 'broad shadow' suggests he would never be able to match his father.

How does the last stanza present the father–son relationship?

The speaker describes how he was 'a nuisance, tripping, falling, / Yapping always', using a tricolon of verbs to build up how useless he felt. The lines also indicate childishness, suggesting he couldn't grow up in his father's presence.

The final lines switch to present tense, 'But today', showing the relationship has changed. The verb 'stumbling' mirrors line 13 but is now linked to his aged father, with the enjambment emphasising his inability to catch up. The images of following are similarly shifted to the father, as is the idea of being a 'nuisance' ('will not go away'). The speaker's tone lacks sympathy and displays exasperation, although his apparent awareness of this may also suggest an admission that he is being unfair.

How does the poem's form contribute to the way meaning is conveyed?

This lyric poem is arranged in six quatrains, mostly in iambic tetrameter (perhaps matching the rhythmic plod of the ploughing) with an *abab* rhyme scheme. This is quite a traditional way of writing, reflecting the father's traditional way of farming and the son wanting to follow in his footsteps.

However, many of the rhymes are actually half-rhymes, representing how the son cannot copy his father. Furthermore, the metre often changes when the speaker remembers his inability to plough like his father. For example, the iambs are replaced with trochees in line 19 (ALL i EVer DID was FOLLow), and line 21 (i WAS a NUIsance, TRIpping, FAlling) ends with an amphibrach. This mirrors the speaker's lack of ploughing skills as a boy, with the final unstressed syllables making the line fade away to show the boy's awkwardness and lack of confidence. It could also represent his rejection of tradition now he's an adult.

Additional context to consider

The poem is autobiographical but has a universal theme of a son trying to move out of the shadow of his father.

Because of the rural setting and the father's skill-set, there is lots of language linked to nature and farming. Many of the words and descriptions are also quite simple or childish because most of the poem looks back to when the speaker was a child.

Poetic links

- Family relationships in 'Walking Away', 'Eden Rock', 'Mother, any distance', 'Before You Were Mine' or 'Climbing My Grandfather'.
- Growing up in 'Walking Away' or 'Mother, any distance'.
- Living in the shadow of a parent in 'Singh Song!'.
- Memories in 'Eden Rock'.

Sample analysis

'Follower' and 'Walking Away' present autobiographical accounts of parent–child relationships. Heaney describes how he admired his father and the simile, 'His shoulders globed like a full sail', shows the effort he put into ploughing. The word 'globed' suggests his arms are wide and his shoulder muscles prominent, with the speaker's childhood perspective linking to why his father seems so big.

In contrast, Day Lewis provides a father's perspective of his son and shows sympathy for his lack of confidence at a new school. Like Heaney, Day Lewis uses a simile, 'Like a winged seed loosened from its parent stem', to present his son's vulnerability. The verb 'loosened' conveys his concern for his son in this new scenario. Images of smallness match the idea of the adult observing the child but the use of the noun 'seed' also implies certainty that the son will grow up and everything will be fine.

Questions

QUICK TEST
1. What causes the speaker to admire his father?
2. Where does the boy appear to feel ignored by his father?
3. What words and phrases show how he feels inadequate?
4. What is the tone of the last sentence?

EXAM PRACTICE
Using one or two of the highlighted quotations to learn, write a paragraph exploring how Heaney presents his father.

MOTHER, ANY DISTANCE
by Simon Armitage

Mother, any distance greater than a single span
requires a second pair of hands.
You come to help me measure windows, pelmets, doors,
the acres of the walls, the prairies of the floors.

5   You at the zero-end, me with the spool of tape, recording
length, reporting metres, centimetres back to base, then leaving
up the stairs, the line still feeding out, unreeling
years between us. Anchor. Kite.

I space-walk through the empty bedrooms, climb
10 the ladder to the loft, to breaking point, where something
has to give;
two floors below your fingertips still pinch
the last one-hundredth of an inch... I reach
towards a hatch that opens on an endless sky
15 to fall or fly.

This poem is about...

a parent–child relationship and the adult child's need for independence.

How does the first stanza present the relationship?

The poem is addressed to the speaker's mother. The opening sentence shows the speaker needing her help, especially in the verb 'requires'. The **idiom** 'second pair of hands' suggests an informal relationship, however, 'Mother' is quite a formal proper noun. This mix of formality could suggest how the relationship is close but strained because of the speaker's need for independence.

Lines 3 and 4 establish the poem's extended metaphor, using a description of the speaker's first house being measured for decorating to represent a child growing up and becoming more independent. The verb 'help' repeats the speaker's dependency and this is emphasised by the list of things that need to be measured: 'windows, **pelmets**, doors'. These features of a room also work on a symbolic level, as they represent a route outside (the speaker's wish for freedom) as well as a barrier (how parents can be restrictive or stifling).

The metaphors, 'the acres of the walls, the **prairies** of the floors', convey a **duality** within the parent–child relationship. The son or daughter is reliant on the parent (needing help to measure up for decoration) but there is an increasing distance between them as the child begins to establish their own life away from home. The metaphors also represent the vast unknown territory of adulthood and the future.

How does the second stanza explore the relationship further?

The extended metaphor is continued. The compound noun 'zero-end' is used to represent birth, while the 'spool of tape' symbolises the **umbilical cord** to suggest that we are always tied to our mothers in some way.

The phrase 'reporting metres, centimetres back to base' uses the verb 'reporting' to show the son or daughter keeps in contact as they move away from home. The phrase 'back to base' indicates a transitional point where the child has moved out, perhaps to university, but still sees the parents' house as their 'base' or home. The phrase 'years between us' presents the mother as staying the same at home while the adult child goes off, changes and experiences new things.

The increasing distance between parent and child is emphasised through verbs and enjambment at the end of lines 6 and 7: 'leaving', 'unreeling'. The final two words of the stanza ('Anchor. Kite.') present another duality: parents are something stable and secure but also something restrictive. The kite, in particular, also conveys the speaker's desire for independence. The short sentences emphasise the significance of the images.

How does the last stanza present the speaker's need for independence?

The 'space-walk' metaphor suggests greater freedom (entering a vast expanse with no gravitational forces) while maintaining the restricting parental link (astronauts are tethered to the spacecraft with what is called an umbilical cable). The 'empty bedrooms' also symbolise the new life the son or daughter will build, indicating a partner and perhaps a child of their own.

The poem uses an imperative verb ('has') to present the adult's need to fully break away from the parent, 'to breaking point, where something / has to give', in order to properly establish their own identity. The shortness of line 11 suggests this action can be frightening and (represented by the empty space on the line) involves a lot of uncertainty. The mother's reluctance to let go of her son or daughter is conveyed in the lines 'two floors below your fingertips still pinch / the last one-hundredth of an inch...', and particularly in the desperate verb 'pinch' and its internal rhyming with 'inch'. The ellipsis creates a tense pause to highlight that this point in life is difficult for both child and parent.

The final lines, 'I reach / towards a hatch that opens on an endless sky / to fall or fly', present the speaker's first steps into full independence. The future's freedom and opportunity is presented through the noun phrase 'endless sky'. The ending depicts the need to leave your parents behind, be independent and make your own mistakes. Like line 11, the brevity of the final line creates uncertainty, highlighted by the rhyming of 'fly' and 'sky'. However, ending with 'fly' rather than 'fall' suggests the speaker's **optimism**.

How does the poem's form contribute to the way meaning is conveyed?

This lyric poem is arranged in three stanzas: two quatrains and a septet. It is written in free verse, helping the poem to resemble normal, everyday speech. However, there are some rhymes (lines 3–4, 5–7 and 14–15) and some of the lines (9, 12 and 13) use iambic pentameter. There is a lot of enjambment but the stanzas are all end-stopped. This varying degree of structure could reflect the mixture of freedom and restriction being depicted in the poem.

The poem looks like a sonnet that lacks its traditional structure of 14 lines, iambic pentameter and a regular rhyme scheme (it was originally published as part of a series of sonnets called *Book of Matches*). This might be a deliberate way of representing the speaker's love for the mother and the simultaneous need to leave her and be independent.

Additional context to consider

The poem presents a common experience through a familiar scenario; the language choices and the use of free verse add to the sense of familiarity. Furthermore, although the poem is addressed to 'Mother', the speaker's gender isn't specified, which allows more readers to empathise and engage with the situation.

Poetic links

- Family relationships in 'Walking Away', 'Eden Rock', 'Follower', 'Before You Were Mine' or 'Climbing My Grandfather'.
- Growing up in 'Walking Away' or 'Follower'.
- The use of extended metaphor in 'Love's Philosophy', 'I think of thee!' or 'Climbing My Grandfather'.

Sample analysis

'Mother, any distance' and 'Follower' present the desire that many young people feel for independence. Armitage matches this common experience with the familiar setting of a house, using the extended metaphor of measuring it for decorating to represent growing up. Describing a 'space-walk through the empty bedrooms' conveys the freedom and adventure of independence, with the 'empty bedrooms' symbolising future possibilities and perhaps linking to the idea of making a family. However, the 'space-walk' also links to parental restriction (as they take place with an umbilical cable) and a child's dependency on their parents.

Heaney also uses metaphor to describe a child's desire for independence. The lines 'All I ever did was follow / In his broad shadow round the farm' use the shadow to represent the son's inability to be his own person due to always trying to live up to his father. This is emphasised with the verb 'follow' and the internal rhyme implying he was always echoing his father.

Questions

QUICK TEST
1. What poetic technique is used throughout the poem?
2. What could the 'spool of tape' symbolise?
3. What is the significance of 'Anchor. Kite.'?
4. How is the mother presented as not wanting to let go of her child?

EXAM PRACTICE
Using one or two of the highlighted quotations to learn, write a paragraph exploring how Armitage presents a parent–child relationship.

BEFORE YOU WERE MINE
by Carol Ann Duffy

I'm ten years away from the corner you laugh on
with your pals, Maggie McGeeney and Jean Duff.
The three of you bend from the waist, holding
each other, or your knees, and shriek at the pavement.
5   Your polka-dot dress blows round your legs. Marilyn.

I'm not here yet. The thought of me doesn't occur
in the ballroom with the thousand eyes, the fizzy, movie tomorrows
the right walk home could bring. I knew you would dance
like that. Before you were mine, your Ma stands at the close
10   with a hiding for the late one. You reckon it's worth it.

The decade ahead of my loud, possessive yell was the best one, eh?
I remember my hands in those high-heeled red shoes, relics,
and now your ghost clatters toward me over George Square
till I see you, clear as scent, under the tree,
15   with its lights, and whose small bites on your neck, sweetheart?

Cha cha cha! You'd teach me the steps on the way home from Mass,
stamping stars from the wrong pavement. Even then
I wanted the bold girl winking in Portobello, somewhere
in Scotland, before I was born. That glamorous love lasts
20   where you sparkle and waltz and laugh before you were mine.

This poem is about...

the speaker's relationship with her mother; she imagines what her mother was like before she was born and feels guilty about how her birth changed her mother's life.

How does the first stanza present the speaker's mother?

The opening phrase, 'I'm ten years away', shows the speaker is imagining what her mother was like 10 years before she gave birth. The poem is addressed directly to her mother.

The mood is of fun and freedom. The verb 'laugh' imagines how happy her mother was, developed by the verb phrase 'shriek at the pavement', which also suggests no **inhibition**. This is emphasised by the image 'Your polka-dot dress blows around your legs. Marilyn.' The single-word sentence acts as a metaphor, comparing her mother to Marilyn Monroe (and a famous, sexy scene from the film *Seven Year Itch* in which her skirt is blown upwards by an air vent) to imply that she was beautiful and glamorous. The reference to specific fashions and films also places this part of the poem in the past.

The informal language ('pals') presents the mother as relaxed and shows she has a close connection with her friends: 'The three of you [...] holding / each other'. The use of proper nouns 'Maggie McGeeney and Jean Duff' makes what the speaker is imagining seem more real.

How does the second stanza develop our impression of the mother?

Like line 1, the phrase 'I'm not here yet' shows the speaker is imagining her mother before she gave birth. This is highlighted by the phrase 'The thought of me doesn't occur', suggesting that she was still carefree.

She describes her mother in 'the ballroom with the thousand eyes', using a metaphor to create an image of a mirrorball while also implying that all the men in the room are attracted to her mother. Another metaphor, 'the fizzy, movie tomorrows / the right walk home could bring', suggests that her mother dreamed of meeting the right man and having a perfect future. This could also indicate that the speaker feels her mother was discontented by the life she actually ended up living.

The poem returns to her mother's carefree attitude, 'your Ma stands at the close / with a hiding for the late one. You reckon it's worth it', showing that mother was told off by her own mother for being late home. The short sentence that ends the stanza adds a little rebelliousness to her character. The colloquial language ('Ma [...] hiding'), like the proper nouns in line 2, adds to the sense of realism.

How does the third stanza present the speaker's feelings?

Again, the stanza opens by looking back to before the speaker was born: 'The decade ahead of my loud, possessive yell was the best one, eh?' The noun phrase 'loud, possessive yell' suggests guilt at taking over her mother's life once she was born. The superlative adjective 'best' indicates the speaker feels her mother thinks her life was ruined; this is emphasised by the use of the rhetorical question and the colloquial form of agreement, 'eh'. This could also be interpreted as gratitude for what they both know her mother sacrificed.

She presents her mother's life of freedom (symbolised by the 'high-heeled red shoes') as being over because of the speaker's birth (showing they are now played with by the child and calling them '**relics**'). She emphasises this through a metaphor, 'your ghost', as if the carefree version of her mother has died. The vividness with which she can imagine her mother's former life (shown through onomatopoeia, 'clatters', and synaesthesia, 'I see you, clear as scent') deepens her sense of guilt.

How does the last stanza explore the mother–daughter relationship?

The speaker presents an image of intimacy, 'You'd teach me the steps', but continues the mood of guilt, 'stamping stars from the wrong pavement'. The adjective 'wrong' (contrasting with 'right' on line 8) shows she thinks her mother should have had a different life, and the metaphor 'stamping stars' could relate to imagining her being a celebrity on the Hollywood Walk of Fame. The speaker introduces the idea that she also wanted to be brought up by the original version of her mother, 'I wanted the bold girl winking', perhaps creating a contrast between this image of rebelliousness and the mother who takes her to church ('Mass').

The final sentence uses a tricolon of verbs to recall the mother's liveliness and happiness, while the repetition of 'before you were mine' emphasises the speaker's feelings of guilt.

How does the poem's form contribute to the way meaning is conveyed?

This lyric poem is written in four quintets in free verse. The poem uses a lot of enjambment but the stanzas are end-stopped. This combination of traditional structure and lack of restraint could mirror the two aspects of the speaker's mother: her carefree life before the speaker was born and her lack of freedom once she becomes a parent.

The free verse also helps the poem to resemble natural speech, linking to how it is addressed to the mother.

Additional context to consider

The poem is autobiographical but the idea of parents sacrificing things to bring up their children is easy to relate to.

It is addressed to Duffy's mother and many details relate specifically to her life, adding a sense of intimacy. The poem isn't bitter, it is loving; while there is a mood of guilt, there is also gratitude and many descriptions praising her mother. Because she loves her mother and is imagining her past (they can't be real memories, it is more like she is looking at old photos), the perspective is unreliable, perhaps idealised or **nostalgic**.

Poetic links

- Family relationships in 'Walking Away', 'Eden Rock', 'Follower', 'Mother, any distance' or 'Climbing My Grandfather'.
- Relationships and thoughts in 'I think of thee!', 'Walking Away', 'Eden Rock' or 'Climbing My Grandfather'.
- Unreliable perspectives of relationships in 'Porphyria's Lover'.

Sample analysis

'Before You Were Mine' and 'Mother, any distance' present contrasting views of parent–child relationships. Duffy suggests that children take over and control their parents' lives. The rhetorical question, 'The decade ahead of my loud, possessive yell was the best one, eh?', suggests her mother was undeniably happier before Duffy was born. The noun phrase 'loud, possessive yell' describes one of the most recognisable aspects of parenthood to convey how babies demand complete attention from their mothers.

Armitage, however, focuses on how parents can be possessive by exploring later years when the child is much less dependent and wants their own life. The lines 'your fingertips still pinch / the last one-hundredth of an inch' emphasise the verb 'pinch' through the internal rhyming with 'inch' to suggest that the mother is desperately holding on to her child. The image of the tape measure symbolises the umbilical cord to highlight this attachment.

Questions

QUICK TEST

1. What is significant about the opening of the first three stanzas?
2. How is the mother presented in the first stanza?
3. Why are the high-heeled shoes called 'relics'?
4. Why is the mother described as a 'ghost'?

EXAM PRACTICE

Using one or two of the highlighted quotations to learn, write a paragraph exploring how Duffy presents her mother.

WINTER SWANS by Owen Sheers

The clouds had given their all –
two days of rain and then a break
in which we walked,

the waterlogged earth
5   gulping for breath at our feet
as we skirted the lake, silent and apart,

until the swans came and stopped us
with a show of tipping in unison.
As if rolling weights down their bodies to their heads

10   they halved themselves in the dark water,
icebergs of white feather, paused before returning again
like boats righting in rough weather.

'They mate for life' you said as they left,
porcelain over the stilling water. I didn't reply
15   but as we moved on through the afternoon light,

slow-stepping in the lake's shingle and sand,
I noticed our hands, that had, somehow,
swum the distance between us

and folded, one over the other,
20   like a pair of wings settling after flight.

This poem is about...

two lovers reuniting after an argument.

How do the first two stanzas present a problem in the relationship?

Pathetic fallacy is used throughout the poem to show the couple's feelings. Weather is used as a metaphor for their argument: 'The clouds had given their all – / two days of rain'. The dash creates a pause, emphasising its severity. The phrase 'and then a break / in which we walked' could suggest a pause from their argument but no reconciliation or could indicate it feels like they have broken up. Enjambment emphasises the divide between them.

The ground is personified as 'waterlogged earth / gulping for breath at our feet' to suggest they cannot communicate. Rain has symbolised their argument so the adjective 'waterlogged' shows it is all they are thinking about. The image of walking through mud represents how they are struggling in their relationship.

The speaker describes how they 'skirted the lake, silent and apart'. The adjectives reinforce their inability to communicate and their feelings of (physical and emotional) separation. The verb 'skirted' means to avoid something, showing they are failing to resolve their argument. The image of the lake could be a metaphor for how deep their problem is or how they haven't been open and transparent with each other.

How do the third and fourth stanzas signal a change in their relationship?

The conjunction 'until' introduces the healing of their relationship. The speaker describes how 'the swans came and stopped us / with a show of tipping in unison'. This shows the couple watched the swans but the verb 'stopped' also represents how the swans saved them from splitting up. The previous images of separation are replaced by one of 'unison'. The reference to how swans dip their heads into water before mating symbolises how the couple are still attracted to each other.

The swans' mating ritual becomes a metaphor for the couple's argument. The image of them 'rolling weights down their bodies to their heads' could suggest the aggression of the couple's argument; 'halved themselves in the dark water' links to how the argument brought the couple close to separation; 'icebergs of white feather' could refer to how the couple have kept apart, as if scared of reigniting their argument; the simile 'returning again / like boats righting in rough weather' suggests the couple are beginning to get past the argument and to steady their relationship.

How do the last three stanzas show the couple repairing their relationship?

The fact about the swans ('They mate for life') is used to suggest that the couple can move beyond their argument and keep their relationship going, suggesting the depth and faithfulness of the couple's love. It is also significant that the couple are speaking again, compared to them being 'silent' in stanza 2. The swans are described as 'porcelain over the stilling water', with the water used as a metaphor to show that things have calmed and their relationship is more secure (a contrast to earlier images of 'rain'); 'porcelain' may imply they are still being careful or that they are aware of how precious their relationship is.

The speaker describes how they 'moved on through the afternoon light'. The reference to their walk is a metaphor for how their relationship has 'moved on' past their argument. The light could also symbolise happiness or a brighter future. Similarly, the ground is now described as 'shingle and sand', suggesting their relationship is steadier (compared to walking on 'waterlogged earth' in stanza 2). However, the verb 'slow-stepping' suggests they are taking things slowly as they begin to get over their argument.

The poem ends with a metaphor for the couple holding hands, showing increased intimacy compared to 'apart' in stanza 2. Their love is presented as instinctive and natural in the way their hands 'somehow, / swum the distance between us', as if this wasn't a deliberate action. The final simile, 'folded, one over the other, / like a pair of wings settling after flight', contains two phrases linked to being a couple or pair and suggests that – like the swans – they will be together forever. The verb 'settling' suggests gentleness while 'after flight' links to the end of their argument.

How does the poem's form contribute to the way meaning is conveyed?

This lyric poem is written in free verse, perhaps to reflect how their argument created disharmony and left their relationship out of shape. The speaker addresses the poem to the lover and it is looking back at past events, so the free verse could also represent the relaxed and open way they now speak, which shows their healthy relationship.

There are seven stanzas: six tercets and a couplet. The final couplet could represent how the couple have got over their argument and come back together, while the tercets could represent how the argument had created a barrier between the couple. The poem also contains a lot of enjambment, perhaps signifying how their relationship keeps going despite their argument.

Additional context to consider

The poem is addressed from the speaker to the lover, creating an intimate mood. Falling out and getting back together again is a familiar experience.

Owen Sheers is a Welsh poet who often writes about the natural landscape in which he was brought up. These natural images appear throughout the poem.

Poetic links

- Romantic love in 'Love's Philosophy', 'I think of thee!' or 'Singh Song!'.
- Intimacy in 'I think of thee!' or 'Singh Song!'.
- Nature imagery in 'Love's Philosophy', 'I think of thee!', 'Neutral Tones', 'The Farmer's Bride' or 'Climbing My Grandfather'.
- A problem in a relationship in 'Love's Philosophy', 'Neutral Tones' or 'The Farmer's Bride'.

Sample analysis

'Winter Swans' and 'The Farmer's Bride' present problems in a relationship. Sheers's lyric poem uses personification, 'the waterlogged earth / gulping for breath at our feet', to present a couple's inability to communicate. Rain has been used as a symbol of their argument so the adjective 'waterlogged' shows that they cannot stop returning to it. The image of walking through mud is also a metaphor for their relationship having difficulty getting beyond this argument.

Mew's dramatic monologue also presents a lack of communication. The farmer says 'I've hardly heard her speak at all. / Shy as a leveret', using the adverb 'hardly' to show how little they talk and italics to suggest he is jealous that she speaks to others. The animal imagery seems natural for a farmer to use but the reference in the simile to a young hare also partly explains the cause of their problem: she is too young and scared of him, and their marriage has confined her like an animal.

Questions

QUICK TEST
1. What is the rain used to symbolise?
2. What is the significance of the swans 'tipping'?
3. How does the 'shingle and sand' represent the couple's relationship?
4. What words or images in the poem link to being a couple?

EXAM PRACTICE
Using one or two of the highlighted quotations to learn, write a paragraph exploring how Sheers uses nature to present the couple's relationship.

SINGH SONG! by Daljit Nagra

I run just one ov my daddy's shops
from 9 o'clock to 9 o'clock
and he vunt me not to hav a break
but ven nobody in, I do di lock –

5   cos up di stairs is my newly bride
vee share in chapatti
vee share in di chutney
after vee hav made luv
like vee rowing through Putney –

10   Ven I return vid my pinnie untied
di shoppers always point and cry:
Hey Singh, ver yoo bin?
Yor lemons are limes
yor bananas are plantain,
15   *dis dirty little floor need a little bit of mop*
in di worst Indian shop
on di whole Indian road –

Above my head high heel tap di ground
as my vife on di web is playing wid di mouse
20   ven she netting two cat on her Sikh lover site
she book dem for di meat at di cheese ov her price –

my bride
she effing at my mum
in all di colours of Punjabi
25   den stumble like a drunk
making fun at my daddy

my bride
tiny eyes ov a gun
and di tummy ov a teddy

30   my bride
she hav a red crew cut
and she wear a Tartan sari
a donkey jacket and some pumps
on di squeak ov di girls dat are pinching my sweeties –

35   Ven I return from di tickle ov my bride
di shoppers always point and cry:
Hey Singh, ver yoo bin?
Di milk is out ov date
and di bread is alvays stale,

40   *di tings yoo hav on offer yoo hav never got in stock*
in di worst Indian shop
on di whole Indian road –

Late in di midnight hour
ven yoo shoppers are wrap up quiet

45   ven di precinct is concrete-cool
vee cum down whispering stairs
and sit on my silver stool,
from behind di chocolate bars
vee stare past di half-price window signs

50   at di beaches ov di UK in di brightey moon –

from di stool each night she say,
How much do yoo charge for dat moon baby?

from di stool each night I say,
Is half di cost ov yoo baby,

55   from di stool each night she say,
How much does dat come to baby?

from di stool each night I say,
Is priceless baby –

This poem is about...

a young Indian man's love for his new wife.

How do the first three stanzas present Singh?

The speaker 'run just one ov my daddy's shops / from 9 o'clock to 9 o'clock'. The poet uses a non-standard form of English, sometimes called Punglish, to present an Indian whose first language is Punjabi. The idea his father keeps him busy is emphasised by 'he vunt me not to hav a break'.

However, he is disobedient – 'ven nobody in, I do di lock' – creating a fun, secretive atmosphere that increases the passion between him and his bride. He describes her 'up di stairs', placing her close but out of sight to increase the sense of desire. At first their behaviour is domestic: 'vee share in di chutney'. This is humorously contrasted with their sexual activity, 'after vee hav made luv / like vee rowing through Putney –', using a simile to suggest the effort they put in. The rhyming of 'chutney' and 'Putney' adds to the humorous tone.

The speaker describes his 'pinnie untied', referring to his sexual activity and perhaps how he feels **emasculated** by his father. His neglect of the shop is described in a funny way, 'Yor lemons are limes / yor bananas are plantain', highlighting how he's more interested in sex.

How do stanzas 4–7 present Singh's bride?

The way the bride's 'high heel tap di ground' above Singh's head suggests he is always thinking about her and could suggest she is in control. This is reinforced by the cat and mouse metaphor in which she appears to run a dating website ('my vife on di web [...] her Sikh lover site'), with verb phrases ('playing wid di mouse [...] netting two cat') showing she can draw in new clients to make money from them ('di cheese ov her price').

Anaphora of 'my bride' focuses the stanzas on Singh's wife and highlights how he adores her. She is headstrong, swearing at his mother ('effing at my mum') and being rude about his father (the simile 'stumble like a drunk / making fun at my daddy'). Her rebelliousness is also in her appearance: 'red **crew cut** / [...] a Tartan sari / a donkey jacket and some pumps' (red can symbolise both danger and love, while **punks** often wore tartan). These images challenge **stereotypes** of Indian brides and their place in the family. Contrasting metaphors suggest the tough and gentle sides of her character: 'eyes ov a gun / and di tummy ov a teddy'.

How do stanzas 8–13 present the relationship between Singh and his wife?

Like stanza 3, the eighth stanza humorously refers to Singh's sexual activities ('di tickle ov my bride') and how this causes him to neglect the shop, repeating the phrase *'di worst Indian shop / on di whole Indian road'*.

The poem ends with the shop taking on a romantic setting, 'di midnight hour / [...] ven di precinct is concrete-cool', through images of darkness and seclusion. Personification ('whispering stairs') and metaphor ('silver stool') create a magical or fairytale backdrop. The shop and its surroundings are described, 'from behind di chocolate bars / vee stare past di half-price window signs / at di beaches ov di UK', using the verb phrase 'stare past' to suggest that because of their love they can ignore their lack of money ('half-price') and luxury ('beaches ov di UK' is a sarcastic description of the streets and gutters).

The speaker relates a nightly conversation he has with his wife, telling her she is twice as 'priceless' as the moon. The adjective conveys how much he adores her and the repeated use of the affectionate noun 'baby' shows this is mutual. The reference to the 'moon' could link to their wishes and hopes for the future. The verb 'charge' could link to their immigrant heritage and suggest that their love makes up for a lack of money and status; it could also suggest how a lack of money might affect their relationship: he is unhappy in the shop but has to work there while she seems less likeable and more calculating when described running her website.

How does the poem's form contribute to the way meaning is conveyed?

This is a dramatic monologue. It is written in free verse and uses non-standard English (the use of Punglish, no full stops and little punctuation within sentences). This helps to create an authentic voice and could reflect the heritage of the speaker as well as how his marriage and his professional life are quite unconventional.

Although the stanzas are different lengths, the last four are couplets. This is perhaps to emphasise the romantic connection being portrayed between the two lovers.

The last words of each line often incorporate rhyme, half-rhyme or alliteration. Inside the lines there are some internal rhymes and regular repetition, alliteration and assonance. These features aren't consistently used to emphasise specific images; instead, they quicken the pace of the poem by making phonological connections between the words. This helps to build up the humorous, happy mood of the poem.

Additional context to consider

The title includes a pun on Singh/sing, indicating that this is a humorous poem. The poem contains wordplay, funny images and a light-hearted tone.

Because it is from the point of view of an Indian with immigrant heritage, the poet has used non-standard English. The speaker is a young man who has just got married so there is also a focus on the new joys of sex. The dramatic monologue creates an intimate, confidential tone.

The poem plays with stereotypes of the Indian community (strictness, modesty, traditional gender roles, strong work ethic, owning 'corner shops', etc.) to create two interesting and unusual characters.

Poetic links

- Romantic love in 'Love's Philosophy', 'I think of thee!' or 'Winter Swans'.
- Intimacy in 'I think of thee!' or 'Winter Swans'.
- Desire in 'Love's Philosophy' or 'The Farmer's Bride'.
- Marriage in 'The Farmer's Bride'.
- Poetic voice in 'Porphyria's Lover' or 'The Farmer's Bride'.

Sample analysis

'Singh Song!' and 'Winter Swans' present love and intimacy. The speaker of Nagra's poem describes how he and his new wife 'made luv / like vee rowing through Putney', and the simile has a light-hearted tone, partly due to it rhyming with 'chutney'. It conveys the young couple's excitement of sex by showing it is very strenuous. The image is quite naughty and matches the confidential tone created by the dramatic monologue.

Sheers uses a more romantic simile for intimacy, matching the lyric style of the poem. The speaker describes he and his partner's hands 'folded, one over the other, / like a pair of wings' to convey gentleness and comfort. The verb 'folded' and the noun 'wings' make them sound protective of their relationship and this is emphasised by the two references to pairs; the comparison to swans also suggests he sees their love as eternal. Both poems are written in free verse, perhaps reflecting how unrestricted their intimacy makes them feel, as shown in the images of rowing and flying.

Questions

QUICK TEST
1. What is unusual about the use of English in the poem?
2. Why is Singh's shop neglected?
3. How does the bride seem unusual?
4. How is the ending of the poem romantic?

EXAM PRACTICE
Using one or two of the highlighted quotations to learn, write a paragraph exploring how Nagra presents the newlyweds.

CLIMBING MY GRANDFATHER
by Andrew Waterhouse

I decide to do it free, without a rope or net.
First, the old brogues, dusty and cracked;
an easy scramble onto his trousers,
pushing into the weave, trying to get a grip.
5   By the overhanging shirt I change
direction, traverse along his belt
to an earth-stained hand. The nails
are splintered and give good purchase,
the skin of his finger is smooth and thick
10   like warm ice. On his arm I discover
the glassy ridge of a scar, place my feet
gently in the old stitches and move on.
At his still firm shoulder, I rest for a while
in the shade, not looking down,
15   for climbing has its dangers, then pull
myself up the loose skin of his neck
to a smiling mouth to drink among teeth.
Refreshed, I cross the screed cheek,
to stare into his brown eyes, watch a pupil
20   slowly open and close. Then up over
the forehead, the wrinkles well-spaced
and easy, to his thick hair (soft and white
at this altitude), reaching for the summit,
where gasping for breath I can only lie
25   watching clouds and birds circle,
feeling his heat, knowing
the slow pulse of his good heart.

This poem is about...

the speaker's memories of his grandfather and the act of remembering.

How do the first four lines introduce the speaker's grandfather?

The opening line establishes the extended metaphor of mountaineering to represent the speaker's grandfather and the process of remembering him. The second half of the line refers to 'free' climbing (not using ropes), suggesting he wants to think freely and open his emotions. The reference to no 'rope or net' indicates this may be emotionally difficult: he risks becoming upset with no one around to comfort him. The idea that remembering is painful implies his grandfather has died. Although the poem is metaphorical, it could also relate to a childhood memory of actually climbing all over his grandad.

Mountaineers start at the foothills, so the speaker begins with his grandfather's shoes: 'First, the old brogues, dusty and cracked'. The adjectives link to age and decay, suggesting how old his grandfather was in his memory but also linking to the idea he has died. He then describes 'an easy scramble onto his trousers, / pushing into the weave, trying to get a grip', with the verb phrases conveying the memory process. It is easy for the speaker to remember but becomes more difficult as he tries to move beyond his grandfather's clothes to think about what he was actually like ('into the weave [...] get a grip').

How do lines 5–12 present the speaker's grandfather?

Verb phrases continue to convey the difficulty of remembering, 'change / direction, traverse along', with the caesura perhaps representing him pausing and searching for his memories. Adjectives describe his grandfather's 'earth-stained hand' and 'splintered' nails, linking him to the outdoors and hard work. These physical attributes help the speaker to build up his memories, conveyed through the continuation of the mountaineering extended metaphor: 'give good purchase', meaning a firm grip.

The description of his nails starts to change the sense from sight to touch. This is emphasised by the adjectives 'smooth and thick' to describe his skin. The speaker adds the simile 'like warm ice', which may show comfort or perhaps symbolise how these more vivid memories begin to upset him and make remembering difficult. Slippery ice would be difficult to climb but the idea of melting could link to him beginning to cry; the oxymoronic phrase could also capture the idea of remembering a dead person ('ice') when they were alive ('warm'). However, he appears to steady himself and continue, 'place my feet / gently [...] and move on'.

How do lines 13–17 present memories and remembering?

The speaker describes his grandfather's 'still firm shoulder'. The adjectives could represent both his grandfather's strength and reliability, and the clearness of this memory. 'Still' could also be an adverb (his shoulder is still firm), creating a mood of pathos that contrasts his grandfather's past physical strength with how weak he became before he died. This sense of sadness could be symbolised by finding himself 'in the shade, not looking down, / for climbing has its dangers'. He uses the verb phrase 'pull / myself up', continuing the mountaineering extended metaphor to suggest he composes himself before continuing with happier thoughts, his 'smiling mouth'.

How do lines 18–27 explore the speaker's feelings?

The adjective 'refreshed' suggests the happy memories are invigorating. The verbs 'stare' and 'watch' suggest a wish to understand his grandfather. Descriptions of age continue, from the metaphor '**screed** cheek' to the noun 'wrinkles' and the reference to his 'white' hair.

His grandfather's head is called 'the summit' and described as if it's in the clouds ('soft and white / at this **altitude**'). As well as continuing the extended metaphor, it shows the speaker's happiness at having constructed this memory; it could also capture how big his grandfather seemed when the speaker was a child. The verb phrase 'gasping for breath' suggests it has been an (emotionally) exhausting experience.

Describing lying down and 'watching clouds and birds circle' creates a peaceful mood that could also link to heaven, suggesting he feels close to his grandfather, emotionally and spiritually. This is emphasised by the final lines, 'feeling his heat, knowing / the slow pulse of his good heart'. While the reference to the heart suggests how he died, the speaker focuses on his grandfather's warmth and goodness; he imagines him still being there and the memory is a comforting presence.

How does the poem's form contribute to the way meaning is conveyed?

This poem is an elegy but it ultimately has a more positive tone than many traditional elegies which tend to focus on grief and loss. It is written in one stanza to suggest a single moment where the speaker thinks about his grandfather. The poet uses enjambment to show how the memories merge into each other and this is also reflected in the use of free verse rather than a structured metre with regular rhyme. Caesuras are increasingly featured to represent the difficulty of remembering (linking to getting out of breath when climbing a mountain).

Additional context to consider

Remembering a loved one is a universal experience and the poet maintains this by focusing on typical features of a grandfather (but in an unusual way through the extended metaphor of mountaineering).

The use of first person adds to the poem's intimacy.

Poetic links

- Nature imagery in 'Love's Philosophy', 'I think of thee!', 'Neutral Tones', 'The Farmer's Bride' or 'Winter Swans'.
- Family relationships in 'Walking Away', 'Eden Rock', 'Follower', 'Before You Were Mine' or 'Mother, any distance'.
- Relationships and thoughts in 'I think of thee!', 'Walking Away', 'Eden Rock' or 'Before You Were Mine'.
- The use of extended metaphor in 'Love's Philosophy', 'I think of thee!' or 'Mother, any distance'.

Sample analysis

'Climbing My Grandfather' and 'Eden Rock' both present how pleasant thoughts of a loved one can be. Perhaps because they refer to the dead, both poems combine an elegiac tone with one of happy nostalgia. Waterhouse's metaphor, 'a smiling mouth to drink among teeth. / Refreshed', recalls the broad smile of the speaker's grandfather. The verb 'drink' and the adjective 'refreshed' suggest that such happy memories can be invigorating while also admitting that the process of remembering is emotionally exhausting.

Similarly, Causley uses a metaphor, 'Her hair, the colour of wheat, takes on the light', to describe the speaker's mother. This gives the mother an almost **celestial** appearance, linking to the idea that she is now dead, heightened by the poem's indication that this is a vision rather than a memory. The light symbolises goodness and perhaps how happy the image makes the speaker feel. Like 'Climbing My Grandfather', the description explores how thoughts of a loved one's physical appearance can reveal their inner character.

Questions

QUICK TEST

1. What extended metaphor is used and what does it describe?
2. How does the use of senses change around lines 7–9?
3. Which words and images suggest remembering can be difficult?
4. How does the end of the poem suggest he feels close to his grandfather?

EXAM PRACTICE

Using one or two of the highlighted quotations to learn, write a paragraph exploring how Waterhouse presents the process of remembering a loved one.

Comparing Poetry

How do I prepare for a comparison of two poems?

It is vital that you specifically compare two poems in your exam answer. You will have one poem in front of you (the one named by the examiner in the question) and will need to pick a suitable poem for comparison from your memory of the other Love and Relationships poems. The exam paper features a list of all the poem titles to help you remember.

It should be easier to find different ideas about the poem that is printed in the paper than from the one you've chosen from memory. For this reason it is a good idea to start by focusing on the poem from your memory and then link it to the poem you've been given, rather than the other way round.

In the exam you need to come up with a quick plan. If you have plenty of revision time, practise planning and writing some poetry essays. Take your time getting used to planning so, by the time it comes to the actual exam, you can do it quickly.

Begin by noting down the quotations that you've learned and thinking about how you can relate them to the exam question. You should also consider whether the title is relevant to the question as this gives you additional language to analyse.

For example:

> Compare how poets present parent–child relationships in 'Mother, any distance' and one other poem.
>
> • 'Before You Were Mine'
>
> How a child takes over a parent's life. Use of possessive pronoun.
>
> • 'shriek at the pavement [...] Marilyn'
>
> Idealised view of her mum; guilt for taking away her freedom. Verb. Single-word metaphor.
>
> • 'in the ballroom with the thousand eyes, the fizzy, movie tomorrows / the right walk home could bring'
>
> Feels mum could have had a better life; also shows she was a romantic dreamer. Metaphor, adjectives, enjambment.
>
> • 'The decade ahead of my loud, possessive yell was the best one, eh?'
>
> Adjectives suggest having a child ruined her life; rhetorical question implies mother and daughter agree.
>
> • 'your ghost clatters toward me over George Square / till I see you, clear as scent'
>
> Metaphor shows she feels she killed her mother's freedom; synaesthesia emphasises her guilt.

Once you've gathered your ideas about your chosen poem, decide what links you can make with the poem named by the examiner. If it helps, you could use a table, as this may be useful for clarifying comparisons and contrasts. For example:

Before You Were Mine	Mother, any distance
1. 'Before You Were Mine' How a child takes over a parent's life. Use of possessive pronoun.	1. 'Mother, any distance' Child wants to escape mother; emotional distance; formal proper noun.
2. 'shriek at the pavement [...] Marilyn' Idealised view of her mum; problem = guilt for taking away her freedom. Verb. Single-word metaphor.	2. 'You come to help me measure windows, pelmets, doors, / the acres of the walls, the prairies of the floors' Extended metaphor; needs her help; problem = emotional / physical distance.
3. 'in the ballroom with the thousand eyes, the fizzy, movie tomorrows / the right walk home could bring' Feels mum could have had a better life; also shows she was a romantic dreamer. Metaphor, adjectives, enjambment.	3. 'the spool of tape / [...] Anchor. Kite.' Metaphors for connection; also suggest speaker feels she is restricting his life.
4. 'The decade ahead of my loud, possessive yell was the best one, eh?' Adjectives suggest having a child ruined her life; rhetorical question implies mother and daughter agree..	4. 'your fingertips still pinch / the last one- hundredth of an inch...' Mother doesn't want him to be independent; verb pinch and sense of desperation emphasised through rhyme.
5. 'your ghost clatters toward me over George Square / till I see you, clear as scent' Metaphor shows she feels she killed her mother's freedom; can't stop focusing on how past has affected present; synaesthesia emphasises her guilt.	5. 'an endless sky / to fall or fly' Verbs to show determination to be independent; unknown future (good or bad) emphasised by rhyme.

You should be able to find similar or contrasting ideas in your two poems; these ideas can form sections of comparison. Look at whether your ideas run in a coherent order and, if not, rearrange them. Ideally, you will have a variety of ideas. However, don't worry if some ideas are similar (as with numbers 3 and 4 above). Use opening words or phrases – such as 'Furthermore...', 'This can also be seen...' and 'Similarly...' – at the start of your paragraphs to suggest this is your way of deliberately developing your point.

While you shouldn't worry about having similar points, try to avoid always analysing the same literary features. The examiner wants a range of understanding so if every paragraph analyses metaphors they won't be impressed. Choose quotations that allow different analysis and, when practising, highlight on your plan the features you're going to explore to make sure they are different.

How do I structure a poetry comparison?

Always start your essay with a very brief introduction. Make sure you clarify which poem you have chosen to use as comparison and try to make a statement that links to the exam question. For example:

> In 'Mother, any distance' and 'Before You Were Mine', Armitage and Duffy present problematic relationships between parents and children. While Armitage's speaker feels his mother is holding him back from being independent, Duffy conveys guilt for having taken away her mother's freedom by being born.

One way of approaching the comparison is to write for 20 minutes about one poem then write for 20 minutes about your second poem. However, you must make sure that, when you write about the second poem, you keep linking your ideas back to the first. You can do this using simple opening phrases like: 'In comparison to 'Mother, any distance'...', 'Like Armitage...', 'Duffy displays a similar idea to Armitage when...' and 'Unlike 'Mother, any distance'...'

A much better way to write your essay is to alternate your paragraphs between the two poems:

Come up with a topic sentence that establishes a point of comparison about the two poems.

Focus on your first poem by clarifying your idea and embedding a quotation.

Analyse how the language of your quotation shows the idea that you have presented. It is better to begin by focusing on language (rather than sentence structure or sounds) as it is primarily words that convey meaning.

Develop your analysis by considering how the language is emphasised by any effects of structure, form or phonology. At this point, you should also consider whether any of the poem's contexts are relevant to the idea you are presenting.

Start a new paragraph. Using a connective of contrast or comparison, introduce your second poem and embed a quotation.

Analyse your second poem in the same way as your first, starting with language and then considering whether any aspects of structure, form, phonology or context could be emphasising the meaning. If you are analysing similar features to your first quotations, make sure you highlight the fact to the examiner as this displays a higher level of comparison.

Starting a new paragraph, come up with a new topic sentence about both poems and repeat the process...

If you're feeling particularly confident in your skills of comparison and analysis, you can try to base your topic sentence round a specific poetic technique. For example: Duffy and Armitage both use metaphor to explore how parent-child relationships can be restricting. This is difficult to sustain for an entire essay so you may just include one or two sections of comparison that have this specific focus on poetic technique.

What does a good section of comparison look like?

If you look back at each of the Love and Relationships poems on pages 4–67, there is a sample section of analysis to help get you thinking about how to compare each poem.

You should try to write fairly equally about the two poems but don't worry about counting up words and making sure it's exact! Try to write in an unhurried and methodical way so you remember to include all the different elements that you need in each section of comparison.

Look at the section of analysis below and annotate it to show how it uses the flow diagram of comparison from page 70.

'Mother, any distance' and 'Before You Were Mine' present the speakers' mixed feelings towards their mothers. Armitage's extended metaphor of measuring a house, 'You come to help me measure windows, pelmets, doors, / the acres of the walls, the prairies of the floors', conveys reliance on the parent through the verb 'help'. However, it also suggests emotional distance through the wall and floor metaphors, with the sense of separation built up by the list. This duality is reinforced by the reference to 'windows, pelmets, doors' – symbols of freedom and restriction that relate to how his mother helps him establish his new life but also wants to keep him at home.

Duffy's poem also uses metaphor to convey mixed feelings. Describing her mother's happy past, 'shriek at the pavement / [...] Marilyn', she compares her to the famous film star as if she was equally beautiful and sexy, using the single-word sentence to represent how she stood out in the crowd. The verb 'shriek' adds a sense of fun and wildness. This more idealised, nostalgic view of the parent links to how the poem is looking back, whereas 'Mother, any distance' is looking forward. However, focusing on the past also highlights the idea that the speaker's mother lost her carefree life, which is emphasised by the fact that Marilyn Monroe died young.

Questions

QUICK TEST
1. Are you allowed to refer to the title of the poem as part of your analysis?
2. Is it better to write one half of your essay on one poem and one half on the other poem, or alternate your paragraphs between the two poems?
3. What is the point of a topic sentence?
4. In each of your paragraphs, what aspect of the poet's writing is it better to analyse first?

EXAM PRACTICE
Looking at the table on page 69, the flow diagram on page 70 and the exemplar above, write another section of analysis comparing how poets present parent–child relationships in 'Mother, any distance' and 'Before You Were Mine'.

1. Compare how poets present the end of a relationship in 'When We Two Parted' and one other poem.

Notes

When We Two Parted

- end not their choice/upsetting
  (re-evaluated in retrospect)
- end presented through natural imagery
- relationship still causes pain

Neutral Tones

- end seemed overdue/deadened emotions
- end presented through natural imagery
- relationship still affects speaker

Both first person and past tense; 19th century values in 'When We Two Parted'; circular vs linear structure.

---

2. Compare the ways poets present attitudes to commitment in 'Love's Philosophy' and one other poem.

Notes

---

3. Compare how poets present a disturbing relationship in 'Porphyria's Lover' and one other poem.

Notes

---

4. Compare how poets present romantic love in 'I think of thee!' and one other poem.

> **Notes**

5. Compare the ways poets present a lack of love in 'Neutral Tones' and one other poem.

> **Notes**

6. Compare the ways poets present a separated relationship in 'Letters from Yorkshire' and one other poem.

> **Notes**

7. Compare how poets use dramatic monologues in 'The Farmer's Bride' and one other poem.

> Notes

8. Compare how poets present family relationships in 'Walking Away' and one other poem.

> Notes

9. Compare how poets explore relationships and thoughts in 'Eden Rock' and one other poem.

> Notes

10. Compare the ways poets present living in the shadow of a parent in 'Follower' and one other poem.

> Notes

11. Compare how poets present attitudes to growing up in 'Mother, any distance' and one other poem.

> Notes

12. Compare the ways poets present an unreliable perspective of a relationship in 'Before You Were Mine' and one other poem.

> Notes

13. Compare the ways poets present a problem in a relationship in 'Winter Swans' and one other poem.

> Notes

14. Compare how poets present intimacy in 'Singh Song!' and one other poem.

> Notes

15. Compare how poets use nature imagery in 'Climbing My Grandfather' and one other poem.

> Notes

Quick tips

- You will get one question on the Love and Relationships poems (plus a question on the Power and Conflict poems if you have studied both collections).

- The examiner will name one poem and it will be printed for you. Read it carefully to fully refresh your memory. You will need to think of a second poem from the Love and Relationships collection that is suitable for comparison.

- Make sure you know what the question is asking you and underline the key words.

- You should spend about 45 minutes on your poetry comparison response. Allow yourself five minutes to plan your answer so there is some structure to your essay.

- All your paragraphs should contain a clear idea, a relevant reference to a poem (ideally a quotation) and analysis of how the poet conveys this idea. Your paragraphs should be linked through comparison and, when relevant, you should link your comments to the poems' contexts.

- It can sometimes help, after each paragraph, to quickly re-read the question to keep yourself focused on the exam task.

- Keep your writing concise. If you waste time 'waffling' you won't be able to include the full range of analysis and understanding that the mark scheme requires.

- It is a good idea to remember what the mark scheme is asking of you...

AO1: Understand and compare the poems (12 marks)

This is all about coming up with a range of points that match the question, supporting your ideas with references from the poems and writing your essay in a mature, academic style.

Lower	Middle	Upper
The essay has some good comparative ideas that are mostly relevant. Some quotations and references are used to support the ideas.	A clear essay that always focuses on the exam question. Quotations and references support ideas effectively. The response includes several comparisons.	A convincing, well-structured essay that answers the question fully. Quotations and references are well-chosen and integrated into sentences. The response provides a detailed and thoughtful comparison of the two poems.

AO2: Analyse effects of the poets' language, structure and form (12 marks)

You need to comment on how specific words, language techniques or sentence structures and the poetic form or metre allow the poets to get their ideas across. To achieve this, you will need to have learned good quotations to analyse.

Lower	Middle	Upper
Identification of some different methods used by the poets to convey meaning. Some subject terminology.	Explanation of the poets' different methods. Clear understanding of the effects of these methods. Accurate use of subject terminology.	Analysis of the full range of the poets' methods. Thorough exploration of the effects of these methods. Accurate range of subject terminology.

AO3: Understand the relationship between the poems and their contexts (6 marks)

For this part of the mark scheme, you need to show your understanding of how the meaning of the poems has been affected by the ways in which they have been written. You could also consider how the meaning of the poems is affected by who wrote them and when they were written.

Lower	Middle	Upper
Some awareness of how ideas are affected by the poems' contexts.	References to relevant aspects of context show a clear understanding.	Exploration is linked to specific aspects of the poems' contexts to show a detailed understanding.

Planning a Poetry Response

How might the exam question be phrased?

A typical poetry comparison question will read like this:

Compare how poets present romance in 'I think of thee!' and one other poem.

[30 marks]

How do I work out what to do?

The focus of this question is clear: the presentation of romance.

'Compare' and 'how' are important elements of this question.

For AO1, 'compare' shows that you need to make a series of structured and well-developed comparisons about romance in the poems. The examiner names one poem and you have to choose a second that is suitable for comparison. Only the poem named in the question will be printed for you; ideally, you should include quotations that you have learned from the other poem but, if necessary, you can make a clear reference to a specific part of the poem.

For AO2, 'how' makes it clear that you need to analyse the different ways in which the poets use language, structure and form to help to show things about romance.

You also need to remember to link your comments to the poems' contexts to achieve your AO3 marks. Think about the way the poems have been written and how this has affected the ways in which meaning is conveyed.

How can I plan my essay?

You have approximately 45 minutes to write your essay.

This isn't long but you should spend the first five minutes writing a quick plan. This will help you to focus your thoughts and produce a well-structured comparative essay.

Try to come up with three or four comparisons (they can be similarities and/or differences). Each of these comparisons can then be written up as a paragraph. For more detailed advice on planning a comparison, look back at pages 68–71.

You can plan in whatever way you find most useful. Some students like to just make a quick list of points and then re-number them into a logical order. Spider diagrams are particularly popular; look at the example on the next page.

'I think of thee!'

Romance = constantly thinking about partner

'my thoughts do twine and bud / About thee'

*context – traditional sonnet addressed to lover

Romance = intimacy (but conveyed implicitly)

'And breathe within thy shadow a new air'

*context – time Barrett Browning was writing; archaic language

Romance = one lover stronger

'And let these bands of greenery which insphere thee / Drop heavily down, – burst, shattered, everywhere!'

Romance = nature imagery

'my palm-tree'

'Singh Song!'

Romance = constantly thinking about partner

'Hey Singh, ver yoo bin? / Yor lemons are limes'

*context – dramatic monologue and focus on humour/subversion

Romance = intimacy

'made luv / like vee rowing through Putney'

*context – time Nagra is writing

Romance = one lover stronger

'effing at my mum / [...] tiny eyes ov a gun / and di tummy ov a teddy'

*context – subversion of gender roles

Romance = nature imagery

'priceless'

*context – shop/shopkeeper links to capitalist Britain rather than religion

Presentation of romance

Summary

- Make sure you know what the focus of the essay is.
- Remember to compare the two poems.
- Remember to analyse how ideas are conveyed by each poet.
- Try to relate your ideas to the poems' contexts.

Questions

QUICK TEST

1. What key skills do you need to show in your answer?

2. What are the benefits of quickly planning your essay?

3. Why is it better to have learned quotations for the exam?

EXAM PRACTICE

Plan a response to the following exam question: Compare how poets present a lack of love in 'Neutral Tones' and one other poem.   [30 marks]

Grade 5 Annotated Response

Compare how poets present romance in 'I think of thee!' and one other poem.

[30 marks]

'I think of thee!' by Elizabeth Barrett Browning and 'Singh Song!' by Daljit Nagra are both about couples and present romantic love (1).

Both poems present romance because the lover is always thinking about their partner. In 'I think of thee!', the whole poem uses nature to show the speaker's thoughts. 'My thoughts do twine and bud / About thee'. The verbs 'twine' and 'bud' suggest her love gets stronger and stronger every time she thinks about him. Because of the verb 'bud', which means to flower, these lines could also show her desire to make love to her partner and have children (2). The regular rhythm emphasises her love and the poem is also a sonnet, which is very romantic (3).

In comparison, 'Singh Song!' is funnier. It shows how the husband is always thinking about his new wife and this is made funny through the speech of his customers. 'Hey Singh, ver yoo bin? / Yor lemons are limes'. This is funny because the description of the fruit shows he neglects the shop. There is internal rhyme and the poet is using Punglish (4). The poem is funnier partly because Daljit Nagra is writing a dramatic monologue about his community, whereas Barrett Browning is writing a sonnet (5).

The two poems explore how people are close together. Barrett Browning's poem is older so it is a bit less upfront than a modern poem. The lines 'Because, in this deep joy to see and hear thee / And breathe within thy shadow a new air, / I do not think of thee – I am too near thee' use the noun 'shadow' to show that they are close together. It is also set at night, which could be quite romantic and suggest they are in bed. The words 'breathe' and 'air' suggest they are kissing and swapping their breath (6).

'Singh Song!' includes references to sex and describes it using a comparison to rowing a boat. This suggests they do it all the time and are really energetic and probably exhausted when they've finished because it's described like exercise. It's funny again and there are rhymes and they have their dinner afterwards which makes Singh sound very happy in love (7).

In the poems, one lover is stronger than the other. In 'I think of thee!', the speaker wants her lover to take control. 'And let these bands of greenery which insphere thee / Drop heavily down, – burst, shattered, everywhere!' This is a metaphor and it uses three words and an exclamation mark to show she is attracted to his strength. Because she wants him to be in charge, she also contrasts a verb where she's in control with one where he takes control and the contrast is highlighted because of the enjambment.

In comparison, Nagra presents Singh's wife as more dominant than her husband. He also uses verbs, contrasts and a metaphor, 'effing at my mum / [...] tiny eyes ov a gun / and di tummy ov a teddy', to show he is attracted to her aggressive, rebellious side as much as her gentle side. The verb 'effing' shows she swears but she's also compared to a teddybear (8).

Both poems use nature images. 'I think of thee!' is full of nature, which shows their love is very natural. She also calls him her 'palm-tree'. This links to religion because on Palm Sunday people have palm trees and this suggests that she worships him. Similarly, Mr Singh compares his wife to the moon, which shows that she is a big part of his universe and also a natural thing. But he can't say how much the moon is worth so he uses the adjective 'priceless', which is really romantic because it shows he loves her more than anything else (9).

1. Clear introduction showing which other poem is being used for comparison. The student could identify how the poems are different in order to establish an argument or exploration. AO1

2. Clear point, evidence and analysis. However, the quotation could be embedded, the expression considered more and subject terminology more sophisticated. AO2

3. Fairly good attempt to develop analysis through form and phonology but understanding could be stronger. AO2

4. A connective is used to clarify comparison. Good choice of quotation but not embedded. Some good analysis but writing could be more concise and varied. Some evidence of feature spotting with the reference to the internal rhyme and use of non-standard English. AO1/AO2

5. Good but not fully successful attempt to develop analysis and include some consideration of context. AO2/AO3

6. Good analysis, although expression could be more precise. Quotation is embedded but it is too long; not all of it is analysed. Some use of context when considering Barrett Browning's language. AO2/AO1/AO3

7. Although comparison is implied, the student needs to make it clear to the examiner. A quotation would be useful to allow analysis and the vocabulary could be less clumsy. AO1/AO2

8. Some good comparison and analysis but explanation could be clearer. AO1/AO2

9. Some good comparison and analysis but expression could be more precise and technical. AO1/ AO2

Questions

EXAM PRACTICE

Choose a paragraph of this essay. Read it through a few times then try to rewrite and improve it. You might:

- improve the sophistication of the language or the clarity of expression

- replace a reference with a quotation or use a better quotation

- ensure quotations are embedded in the sentence

- provide more detailed, or a wider range of, analysis

- use more subject terminology

- link some context to the analysis more effectively.

Grade 7+ Annotated Response

A proportion of the best top-band answers will be awarded Grade 8 or Grade 9. To achieve this, you should aim for a sophisticated, fluid and nuanced response that displays flair and originality.

Compare how poets present romance in 'I think of thee!' and one other poem.

[30 marks]

'I think of thee!' presents a more traditional image of romance between a man and a woman than 'Singh Song!', although both explore ideas of love, desire and gender roles (1).

Both poems present romantic constancy through the image of a lover always thinking about their partner. In 'I think of thee!', this is achieved through the extended metaphor of a tree and a vine. The lines 'my thoughts do twine and bud / About thee' present the speaker's romantic thoughts as a vine wrapping itself around the lover. The verbs 'twine' and 'bud' suggest her love grows every time she thinks about him and could show her desire to make love to her partner and have children. The regular iambic pentameter mirrors this steady growth of her love (2).

In comparison, 'Singh Song!' conveys the husband's constant focus on his new wife through humour (3). The italicised speech of his customers, 'Hey Singh, ver yoo bin? / Yor lemons are limes', indicates he neglects the shop because he's always with or thinking about her. Humour is created by combining internal rhyme and the poet's use of Punglish with the subversion of the stereotype of a hardworking Indian son. The difference in tone between the poems is partly linked to how Nagra is writing a dramatic monologue that explores his community, whereas Barrett Browning's sonnet is more traditional and addressed to her lover (4).

The two poems explore the role of intimacy in romance. Due to the time in which it was written, Barrett Browning's images are more ambiguous than Nagra's. The line 'And breathe within thy shadow a new air' can be interpreted as showing their love is like a fresh start. However, the use of the noun 'shadow' indicates closeness and the line could be a sensual description of them sharing each other's breath at night (5).

In contrast, 'Singh Song!' features the risqué simile 'made luv / like vee rowing through Putney' to suggest the effort that the couple put into their love-making. Humour is again created by rhyming 'Putney' with the earlier 'chutney'. Whereas Barrett Browning presents her sonnet as a piece of classical literature, older than it actually is, by using archaic language like 'thy', Nagra's poem is more modern, which explains the greater explicitness (6).

Romance is also explored in the poems by having one lover as stronger than the other. In 'I think of thee!', the speaker initially seems stronger but yearns for her lover to take control. When she says 'And let these bands of greenery which insphere thee / Drop heavily down, – burst, shattered, everywhere!', the tricolon of broken images suggests she is attracted to his strength and this is emphasised by the exclamation mark. The wish for him to be in charge is also shown through the contrasting verb phrases and the way they are highlighted by the enjambment.

In comparison, Nagra plays with gender roles by clearly presenting Singh's wife as more dominant. Like Barrett Browning, Nagra shows this dominance through verb phrases, contrasts and metaphor. The lines 'effing at my mum / [...] tiny eyes ov a gun / and di tummy ov a teddy' show that the speaker appreciates the aggressive, rebellious side of his bride as much as her gentleness. The strength of his love could be reflected in the way the alliteration highlights her cuter characteristics (7). However, it could be argued that Barrett Browning is also inverting gender roles in her poem as it was more traditional for male poets to be the ones writing passionate sonnets to their lovers (8).

Despite their different tone and style, linking to their different cultural and historical contexts, 'I think of thee!' and 'Singh Song!' are both very romantic poems. This is perhaps best shown through their use of nature images. Barrett Browning's speaker refers to her lover as 'my palm-tree', using religious imagery to suggest that she worships him. Similarly, Nagra's speaker compares his wife to the moon but (relating to the speaker being a shopkeeper in modern Britain) focuses on capitalism rather than religion, using the adjective 'priceless' to convey just how much he values her (9).

1. Clear introduction, establishing a sense of comparison and argument. AO1
2. Good paragraph of analysis, using embedded quotations and providing sophisticated analysis of language and form. A range of subject terminology is applied accurately. AO2
3. Clear sense of comparison. AO1
4. Good use of context, firmly linked to the surrounding analysis. AO3
5. Some sophisticated language choices and strong analysis. AO1/AO2
6. Good use of context, although it could be developed further. AO3
7. Exploratory analysis and comparison, strengthened by exploring the effects of structure and form. AO1/AO2
8. Context used to provide alternative interpretation. AO3
9. Good conclusion, highlighted by additional close comparison of language and consideration of context. AO1/AO2/AO3

Questions

EXAM PRACTICE

Spend 45 minutes writing an answer to the following question:

Compare how poets present a lack of love in 'Neutral Tones' and one other poem. [30 marks]

Remember to use the plan you have already prepared.

Glossary

Glossary of literary terms

Abstract noun – an idea or feeling rather than an object

Adjective – a word to describe a noun

Adjective phrase – a series of words making up an adjective

Adverb – a word to describe a verb

Adverbial phrase – a series of words making up a description of a verb

Alliteration – a series of words beginning with the same sound

Allusion – a reference to something without specifically stating it

Anaphora – repeating words or phrases in a structured way (such as at the start of stanzas)

Assonance – repetition of **vowel sounds** inside a series of words

Caesura – a pause within a line of poetry, created by a punctuation mark

Clauses – grammatical units (sets of words) separated by punctuation

Colloquial – everyday, informal language

Comparative adjective – an adjective that shows comparison (e.g. bigger, quieter, better)

Compound noun – two words joined together by a hyphen to create a noun

Conjunction – a linking word such as and, but or while

Dramatic monologue – a poem in which the poet takes on the voice of a character and addresses an imagined audience

Elegy – a poem of serious reflection, often focusing on grief due to the death of a loved one

Ellipsis – punctuation (…) used to indicate words that have been missed out

End-stopped – using punctuation (such as a comma, full stop or dash) at the end of a line of poetry

Enjambment – continuing a sentence across lines of poetry without end-stopping

Euphemism – replacing a harsh or taboo word or phrase with a milder, more indirect one

Exclamative – a phrase or sentence that conveys strong emotion

Extended metaphor – a metaphor that is continued throughout a series of images

First person – using I (singular) or we (plural) to show a personal or shared experience

Foreshadowing – suggesting something that is going to happen later

Half-rhyme – a near rhyme, needing one **vowel sound** to change to achieve a full rhyme

Hyperbole – exaggerated language

Imagery – descriptive language (images, simile, metaphor, personification)

Imperative – a sentence or word that contains an order

Indefinite article – an article introduces a noun; they are either definite (the) or indefinite (a, an)

Internal rhyme – words that rhyme within lines of poetry (rather than at the ends of lines)

Irony – saying one thing in order to deliberately suggest the opposite; a situation that appears deliberately the opposite of what you might expect

Juxtaposition – placing two things next to each other, usually to create a contrast

Lyric poem – a formal poem, usually in the first person, expressing powerful, personal emotions

Melancholy – a feeling of thoughtful sadness

Metaphor – a descriptive technique, using comparison to say one thing is something else

Mood – the dominant emotion or atmosphere of a piece of writing

Noun – a word indicating an object

Noun phrase – a series of words making up a noun

Onomatopoeia – words that sound like the sound they are describing

Oxymoron – a phrase created by words with apparently opposite meanings

Parallelism – repetition of a grammatical structure (often with one small change) for effect

Pathetic fallacy – the use of nature, such as weather, to reflect human emotions

Personification – describing an object or idea as if it has human characteristics

Phonology – sounds within speech

Plosives – harsh sounds formed through a sudden release of air from the mouth

Pronoun – a word used as a substitute for a noun; personal pronouns show who is speaking (I, he, she, they); possessive pronouns indicate ownership (my, her, their); singular and plural pronouns indicate whether one or more person is involved (I/they)

Proper noun – a name of a person, place, organisation, etc.

Pun – the humorous effect of using words that sound similar but have different meanings

Repetition – saying something more than once to achieve a specific effect

Rhetorical question – a question used to make the listener think, rather than gain an answer

Rhyme – words with the same sound (patterns of rhyme can be noted using letters, so *abab* shows that the first and third lines of a poem rhyme, as do the second and fourth lines)

Second person – writing using the pronoun 'you' (as opposed to **first person** or third person)

Sibilance – repetition of s sounds

Simile – a descriptive technique, using like or as to form a comparison

Sonnet – a 14-line poem in iambic pentameter with a fixed rhyme scheme, usually focusing on love

Stanza – a group of lines in a poem (like a paragraph of poetry)

Superlative adjective – an adjective that shows the most something can be (e.g. biggest, quietest, best)

Symbol – an object or colour used to represent a different meaning

Synaesthesia – using one sense to describe another sense

Third person – writing using the pronouns he, she or they (as opposed to **first person**, I)

Tone – the way words suggest a particular mood or feeling

Tricolon – ideas or words arranged into a pattern of three for a specific effect

Verb – a doing or action word

Verb phrase – a series of words making up a verb

Vowel sounds – the sounds created when pronouncing vowels; these can be short (a, e, i, o, u) or long (A, E, I, O, U, OO, AH)

Wordplay – exploiting the ambiguous meanings of words, for example through **puns**

Metre

Metre – the rhythmic structure of a line of poetry, based on patterns of stress, created through the type and number of metrical feet it contains; if a line uses two feet it is dimeter, three feet is trimeter, four feet is tetrameter, five is pentameter, etc.

Foot – a unit of rhythm, containing stressed and/or unstressed beats (plural = feet)

Iamb – this is the most regularly used metrical foot; it consists of an unstressed beat followed by a stressed beat

Iambic tetrameter – a line consisting of four iambs

Iambic pentameter – a line consisting of five iambs

Trochee – a metrical foot consisting of a stressed beat followed by an unstressed beat

Trochaic tetrameter – a line consisting of four trochees

Amphibrach – a metrical foot consisting of an unstressed beat, then a stressed beat then another unstressed beat

Anapaest – a metrical foot consisting of two unstressed beats followed by a stressed beat

Cretic – a metrical foot consisting of a stressed beat, followed by an unstressed beat then another stressed beat

Blank verse – a poem that uses a specific metre (often iambic pentameter) but doesn't use a set rhyme scheme

Free verse – a poem that uses neither a specific metre nor a set rhyme scheme

General glossary

Abstract – related to ideas and theories rather than specific events or objects

Altitude – the height of something above sea-level; a great height

Ambiguous – unclear, open to interpretation

Archaic – ancient, no longer used

Beseech – beg

Betwixt – between

Brevity – shortness

Celestial – linked to heaven and immense goodness

Classical – relating to ancient Greek or Latin literature

Conform – follow rules or expectations

Connotation – suggested meaning

Convention – expected ways of behaviour

Courtship – a period when a couple go on dates to establish their relationship

Crew cut – a very short haircut, associated with men

Despondent – feeling low, down-hearted

Disdain – treat without respect

Domesticity – things related to home and family life

Duality – the quality of being double

Emasculate – to remove a man's feeling of masculinity

Erotic – creating or relating to sexual desire

Fay – fairy

Femininity – qualities that are linked to being female

Fledged – when a bird has developed wing feathers large enough to enable flight

Foreground – bring to the front; make something more prominent

Idealised – an unrealistically perfect view of something

Idiom – a familiar phrase or saying

Inhibition – feeling self-conscious and unable to relax

Jargon – specialist words linked to a particular subject

Knell – the sound of a bell, usually being rung to announce a death or funeral

Linear – arranged in a straight line

Manic – having abnormally heightened moods (such as happiness or anger), leading to unpredictable behaviour and delusions

Mortality – being subject to death, as opposed to living forever

Necrophilia – attraction to, or sexual intercourse with, a corpse

Nostalgic – viewing the past in an overly positive way

Objectify – treat someone like an object rather than a valued individual

Ominous – suggesting something bad will happen

Optimism – positive outlook; hopefulness about the future

Pathos – creating great sympathy or sadness

Pelmet – a border across the top of a window or door

Platonic – love between friends that is affectionate rather than sexual

Prairie – a large area of grassland

Punks – followers of punk music, linked to aggression and being anti-establishment

Quatrain – a four-line **stanza**

Relic – an object from a previous time period, often found in a museum

Repress – prevent; hold back

Rue – regret

Rural – related to the countryside

Screed – made up of scree, loose stones covering a mountain slope

Sensual – related to the senses and/or sexual pleasure

Stereotype – an oversimplified view of a group of people that is widely held in society

Subconsciously – taking place in, or influenced by, the mind without full awareness

Subvert – undermine established thought; flip the expected way of doing something

Surreal – dreamlike and strange

Thrift – taking care with money rather than being wasteful

Umbilical cord – the cord (carrying oxygen and nutrients) that connects a baby to its mother when in the womb

Vex – to annoy or frustrate

Victorian – relating to the period of British history when Queen Victoria reigned (1837–1901)

Woo – try to gain someone's love; chat-up

Answers

Pages 4–7: 'When We Two Parted'

QUICK TEST

1. On line 2 they suggest unhappiness at parting and not being able to find the right words; on the last line they link to unhappiness at the lover's betrayal and not wanting to speak to the lover.
2. 'It felt like the warning / Of what I feel now'.
3. Fame, spoken, name.
4. 'Long, long shall I rue thee'.

EXAM PRACTICE

Ideas might include the way 'silence and tears' is changed between the start and the end, or the suspicion that could be included in 'Half broken-hearted'; the metaphor for being betrayed; the bell metaphor suggests it almost kills him to hear about her; the accusing metaphors, the switching from a plural to singular pronoun to show separation, the effect of the individual verbs, and the use of parallelism for emphasis.

Pages 8–11: 'Love's Philosophy'

QUICK TEST

1. Love is natural or normal.
2. Love is holy and moral.
3. Rhetorical question.
4. Mingle, mix, kiss, clasp.

EXAM PRACTICE

Ideas might include the use of nature imagery to present love as normal, and religious references to present it as moral; the use of stronger images representing men and weaker images representing women suggests a traditional view of gender roles in relation to love; the 'sunlight' metaphor suggests how much he needs the woman and implies (through the idea of the Earth orbiting the Sun) that he can't resist her; the final rhetorical question suggests that love gives meaning to everything else in the world.

Pages 12–17: 'Porphyria's Lover'

QUICK TEST

1. She seems almost magical (perhaps suggesting this is the speaker's fantasy); she is a source of warmth and happiness.
2. The pathetic fallacy, his obsessive tone and the murder imply he is mentally disturbed.
3. Her yellow hair.
4. She would have been glad because he has freed her from the things that restricted her and given her a better life.

EXAM PRACTICE

Ideas might include the verb 'glided' suggesting this is the speaker's fantasy vision of Porphyria; the bare shoulder and the repeated descriptions of her hair present her as sensual to convey the speaker's sexual obsession; his probably misplaced belief that she 'worshipped' him and the metaphor 'Made my heart swell' include exaggerated language to show his obsession; the metaphor and alliterated plosives show him kissing her dead lips aggressively and, at the end, the verb 'gained' suggests he thinks she is happy to have been murdered because now she can be with him always.

Pages 18–21: Sonnet 29 – 'I think of thee!'

QUICK TEST

1. The speaker is the vine; the man is the tree.
2. Their love is spiritual as well as physical; she worships him.
3. His actual physical presence.
4. He makes her happier; it is almost like he is bringing her back to life.

EXAM PRACTICE

Ideas might include how the metaphor suggests she cannot stop thinking about him and her every thought makes her love stronger; the imperative and the adverb suggest she's desperate to see him again while the noun 'presence' suggests she worships him; the contrast of 'insphere' and 'drop', followed by the tricolon of broken images, suggests she wants to give herself to him utterly and be dominated by him; the noun phrase and the tricolon of verbs suggests the enjoyment of being with him, which is emphasised by the idea ('new air') that he brings her to life.

Pages 22–25: 'Neutral Tones'

QUICK TEST

1. The cold, empty descriptions of the setting are used to mirror the speaker's own emptiness and lack of emotion.
2. Lack of communication.
3. Love deceives.
4. Colours: white and grey. Indefinite articles (a tree, a pond, instead of the). Lack of description and few words linked to strong emotion.

EXAM PRACTICE

Ideas might include how the pathetic fallacy uses images of cold to suggest that his emotions have been blunted by his experiences; images of nature (traditionally used to present love) are subverted to show love dying; personification suggests they didn't take enough care of their relationship; the contrast of 'smile' and 'deadest' show how much the relationship has changed; the metaphor also suggests that they pretend everything's okay and perform their relationship even though it's over, while the word 'thing' suggests they come to repulse each other; the ending of the relationship still hurts and the personification 'love deceives' shows it has left him cynical about love.

Pages 26–29: 'Letters from Yorkshire'

QUICK TEST

1. He seems more active with more time spent outdoors; his pace of life seems slower but freer; there is a suggestion that she is less satisfied with her life.
2. It's not a romantic relationship.
3. 'came / indoors to write to me', 'sends me word of that other world / pouring air and light into an envelope', 'watching the same news in different houses, / our souls tap out messages'.
4. Separating the sentences across the tercets represents something that is together yet distanced.

EXAM PRACTICE

Ideas might include how 'indoors' represents her lifestyle, linking with the verb 'write' to show him reaching out to her, as well as the way she imagines how he feels miles away; the enjambment separates 'you' and 'me' although they are in the same sentence; the metaphor represents part of Yorkshire travelling across the country to the speaker, as well as the enjoyment she gets from his letters; the contrast between the adjectives 'same' and 'different', plus the metaphor for their spiritual or subconscious connection.

Pages 30–34: 'The Farmer's Bride'

QUICK TEST

1. The farmer's use of the verb 'chose' and the fact there was no courtship.
2. The bride's fear of men and, in particular, sex.
3. A hare (a leveret is also a hare) and a mouse.
4. Children and sex with his wife.

EXAM PRACTICE

Ideas might include his lack of interest in romance, the way he 'chose' her (presumably as someone sexually attractive who he also thought would be a good, dutiful wife) and his regret that in hindsight she was too young; the verb phrases implying ownership; repetition, exclamation and verbs to show her fear contrasted with his apparent ignorance of why she is scared; adjectives linked to physical appearance, alongside exclamation, repetition and short clauses show his frustrated sexual desire for her.

Pages 35–38: 'Walking Away'

QUICK TEST

1. 'like a satellite / wrenched from its orbit'; 'Like a winged seed loosened from its parent stem'.
2. The description of going to school in lines 8–12. The speaker feels sorry for his son ('pathos') and is aware he isn't ready ('half-fledged'); the boy seems vulnerable ('wilderness [...] eddying away / Like a winged seed') and uncertain ('finds no path where the path should be [...] hesitant').
3. The clay-baking metaphor: 'the small, the scorching / Ordeals which fire one's irresolute clay'.
4. Sacrifice and love.

EXAM PRACTICE

Ideas might include how the verb 'wrenched' shows it is painful to see the son moving away; the noun 'pathos' shows he feels sorry for his son; his tenderness is shown in the adjective 'half-fledged', which also shows he worries about his son and this is emphasised by the enjambment before 'Into a wilderness'; the clay-baking metaphor shows he has put up with emotional pain in order to prepare his son, and himself, for independence; the verb phrase 'letting go' is presented as the greatest act of love and sacrifice.

Pages 39–42: 'Eden Rock'

QUICK TEST

1. It is specific (the proper noun, even though it's fictional) yet vague ('somewhere').
2. Femininity through nature and the focus on her pretty appearance; domesticity through the way she arranges the picnic and serves the tea.
3. 'takes on the light', 'sky whitens as if lit by three suns', 'drifted stream'.
4. They appear to be comforting him and guiding him to the afterlife.

EXAM PRACTICE

Ideas might include how he appears to be imagining them in a perfect afterlife; his mother is a traditional image of femininity (linked to nature) but also dreamlike, maybe celestial ('takes on the light'); his mother is linked to calm (the adverb 'slowly') and domesticity, while the 'three plates' suggest he feels his parents are calling to him to join them; the verb 'beckon' suggests they are guiding and comforting him as he approaches death, it also implies he may be looking forward to joining them again; comfort also appears in how they seem to present dying as nothing to fear.

Pages 43–46: 'Follower'

QUICK TEST

1. His strength and skill with a plough.
2. Not feeling part of the team and his father keeping his eyes on the ground.
3. Stumbled, fell, to his plod, follow in his broad shadow, nuisance, tripping, falling, yapping.
4. Unsympathetic and exasperated.

EXAM PRACTICE

Ideas might include the simile to show his strength and the childhood perspective of his size; the short sentence emphasises the son's admiration for his father's skills but also links to his simple way of life; verbs (narrowed, angled, mapping) and adverbs (exactly) show skill but the reference to looking at the ground suggests he feels ignored by his father; the shadow metaphor suggests he can't compete with his father and wants to get away from him; the shifting of previous images from the son to the father show role reversal but it's not sympathetic and has a tone of exasperation.

Pages 47–50: 'Mother, any distance'

QUICK TEST

1. Extended metaphor.
2. The umbilical cord (also alluded to on line 9).
3. The two images show how a parent is both caring and restrictive. They show safety and security but no freedom. The kite in particular also shows the child's desire for independence.

4. The verb 'pinch' and its internal rhyming with 'inch', showing the mother not wanting to let go of the tape measure. The ellipsis that follows suggests that letting go is difficult for the mother and the child.

EXAM PRACTICE

Ideas might include the use of the extended metaphor to show a child growing up; the description of measuring to show the child's dependency but also them moving away from the parent, plus the features of the room symbolising both freedom and restriction; the metaphor for the umbilical cord suggesting children are always linked to their mothers; the 'Anchor. Kite.' image, showing how parents are caring yet restrictive, while children want freedom, and the emphasis of this through the short sentences; the verb 'pinch' and its internal rhyming with 'inch' to suggest parents never want to let their children go, plus the ellipsis to show it's a difficult situation.

Pages 51–54: 'Before You Were Mine'

QUICK TEST

1. The opening phrases take the poem back in time to before the speaker was born.
2. Happy, carefree, uninhibited. The speaker compares her to a beautiful, glamorous film star, although this may link to the idea of imagination and the speaker's unreliable perspective.
3. Her mother no longer gets dressed up and goes out so the shoes are old and unused, like things from a former time sitting in a museum.

4. The metaphor suggests that her mother's former, carefree life (not her mother herself) has died.

EXAM PRACTICE

Ideas might include how her mother's happiness and lack of inhibition is shown through verbs and how this is emphasised by the metaphor comparing her to Marilyn Monroe; the Monroe comparison could also suggest that the speaker's perspective is unreliable (linking to how these aren't real memories); the mirrorball metaphor shows her mother liked to go out but also suggests she was very attractive as all the men were watching her; it suggests she was a romantic who dreamed of a fairytale future (but the use of 'right' implies the speaker feels guilty for it turning out differently); the 'ghost' metaphor shows that her mother's old carefree life is dead; the onomatopoeia and synaesthesia show how vividly the speaker can imagine the life her mother has lost, deepening the sense of guilt.

Pages 55–58: 'Winter Swans'

QUICK TEST

1. Their argument.
2. It is a mating ritual, suggesting the couple are still attracted to each other.
3. It suggests a steadier relationship (compared to the 'waterlogged' mud in stanza 2).
4. We, our, us, unison, folded one over the other, pair of wings.

EXAM PRACTICE

Ideas might include the pathetic fallacy throughout the poem to show their changing feelings; the 'waterlogged earth' as a metaphor for their inability to escape their argument and move on; the verb 'skirted' showing they aren't resolving the problem and being transparent with each other; the swans being used as a metaphor for the couple's relationship and the 'tipping' showing that they are still attracted to each other; the 'afternoon light' symbolising happiness and the 'shingle and sand' being a stronger foundation for their relationship compared to the 'waterlogged earth'; the 'pair of wings' representing how they are back together and, like the swans, will be partners forever.

Pages 59–63: 'Singh Song!'

QUICK TEST

1. It is written in non-standard English to show the speaker's mix of English and Punjabi.
2. He would rather spend time with his wife, ideally making love.
3. She seems in control of the relationship, she's headstrong and rebellious.
4. He tells her that she is twice as priceless as the moon and they call each other baby.

EXAM PRACTICE

Ideas might include the simile for sex showing they are passionate; the verb 'effing' could suggest disapproval or amusement but the line shows that family isn't an obstacle to their love; the contrasting metaphors show that he loves both sides of her character (the good and the bad); the personification and metaphor suggest that when they're alone it's magical or like a fairytale, even though they're still in the shop; the adjective 'priceless' suggests that his love is infinite and the repeated use of 'baby' shows their love is mutual.

Pages 64–67: 'Climbing My Grandfather'

QUICK TEST

1. Extended metaphor of mountaineering. It describes his grandfather's appearance as well as the process of remembering.
2. As well as sight, the poem begins to include touch.
3. Without a rope or net, pushing, trying, warm ice, rest for a while in the shade, climbing has its dangers, pull myself up, refreshed, cross the screed cheek, gasping for breath.
4. The speaker describes being able to feel his grandfather's heat and pulse; it is like he has felt his grandfather's presence.

EXAM PRACTICE

Ideas might include how the change of verb phrases suggests remembering can be difficult and emotionally exhausting, especially when moving beyond basic appearances to what someone was actually like; the simile suggests vivid memories (such as those linked to senses other than sight) can be upsetting; the verb 'drink' and the adjective 'refreshed' also suggest that remembering can be exhausting while the metaphor conveys how a happy memory can be invigorating; the verb 'feeling' and the nouns 'heat' and 'pulse' suggest memory can be so strong it almost brings that person back.

Pages 68–71: Comparing Poetry

QUICK TEST

1. Yes, the title can provide you with extra language to analyse.
2. Alternate paragraphs.

3. It establishes a point of comparison about the poems, showing the examiner that you are meeting the assessment criteria.
4. Start by focusing on language then consider how meaning is emphasised by structure, form or phonology.

EXAM PRACTICE

Using the flow diagram on page 70, check that your section follows the comparison structure.

Pages 75–76: Planning a Poetry Response

QUICK TEST

1. Comparison of the two poems, specific analysis and terminology, awareness of the relevance of context, a well-structured essay.
2. Planning focuses your thoughts and allows you to produce a well-structured essay.
3. Quotations give you more opportunities to do specific AO2 analysis.

EXAM PRACTICE

Poem choices for comparison would include 'When We Two Parted', 'Love's Philosophy' or 'The Farmer's Bride'. Ideas for the comparison might include how the speaker lacks love, what has caused the lack of love, how this feeling is described, and how the speaker responds to the lack of love.

Pages 77–80: Graded Responses

EXAM PRACTICE

Use the mark scheme to self-assess your strengths and weaknesses. Work up from the bottom, putting a tick by things you have fully accomplished, a ½ by skills that are in place but need securing, and underlining areas that need particular development. The estimated grade boundaries are included so you can assess your progress towards your target grade.

Grade	AO1 (12 marks)	AO2 (12 marks)	AO3 (6 marks)
6–7+	A convincing, well-structured essay that answers the question fully. Quotations and references are well-chosen and integrated into sentences. The response provides a detailed and thoughtful comparison of the two poems.	Analysis of the full range of the poets' methods. Thorough exploration of the effects of these methods. Accurate range of subject terminology.	Exploration is linked to specific aspects of the poems' contexts to show a detailed understanding.
4–5	A clear essay that always focuses on the exam question. Quotations and references support ideas effectively. The response includes several comparisons.	Explanation of the poets' different methods. Clear understanding of the effects of these methods. Accurate use of subject terminology.	References to relevant aspects of context show a clear understanding.
2–3	The essay has some good comparative ideas that are mostly relevant. Some quotations and references are used to support the ideas.	Identification of some different methods used by the poets to convey meaning. Some subject terminology.	Some awareness of how ideas are affected by the poems' contexts.